Praise for Watsamatta U

Like the b
many leve
family dia
blessings
lege. You
end you v
book. You

This book
with an a
temporari

Take this
having yo

Watsamatta U:

A Get-a-Grip Guide to Staying Sane Through Your Child's College Application Process

Watsamatta U:

A Get-a-Grip Guide to Staying Sane Through Your Child's College Application Process

Karin Kasdin

Chandler House Press
Worcester, Massachusetts

Watsamatta U: A Get-a-Grip Guide to Staying Sane Through Your Child's College Application Process

Copyright © 2002 by Karin Kasdin

Watsamatta U: A Get-a-Grip Guide to Staying Sane Through Your Child's College Application Process

ISBN 1-886284-71-7

Library of Congress Card Number: 2002102714
First Edition

ABCDEFGHIJK

Published by
Chandler House Press, Inc.
A division of Tatnuck Bookseller & Sons, Inc.
335 Chandler Street
Worcester, MA 01602
USA

President
Lawrence J. Abramoff

Director of Publishing
Claire Cousineau

Cover, Interior Design, and Production
CWL Publishing Enterprises
Madison, WI, www.cwlpub.com

Chandler House Press publishes nonfiction and reference books. For more information on special sales, publishing opportunities, or distribution channels, please contact Chandler House Press, 335 Chandler Street, Worcester, MA 01602. Call (800) 642-6657 or (508) 756-7644, fax (508) 756-9425, or find us on the World Wide Web at www.chandlerhousepress.com.

Contents

Dedication

This book is dedicated to my firstborn son, Dan.

For your generosity of spirit in letting me share our story, for your unflagging sense of humor through a process that could have killed the both of us, for your acceptance of your role as guinea pig as I continue to learn how to parent, and most of all for your love, which is among my greatest gifts.

Preface

As any author knows, it can take anywhere from one year to the rest of your life to get a book published. In my case it took a year and a half from the time I typed the last word on my computer to the time I will read the first word in book form. In that year and a half the son about whom this book is written has become a sophomore in college. He made a smooth transition to college life. I'm sure the beer helped. (I am nothing if not honest.) He is a happy young man. And me? Let's just say that my Estée Lauder moisturizer and concealer are working twice as hard for half the results they obtained before the college chase carved permanent grooves in my face.

I became a lunatic during my son's college application process. He would argue that I was obsessed with college long before the application process officially began. Perhaps he's right. Achievement has, until recently, been a motivating force in my life. And even now, I can't lie and say that I've conquered the achievement demon. If I had I wouldn't have been compelled to write this book.

I write it not only for achievement's sake, however. I write with candor about the worst in me that was brought to the surface as I tried to "launch" my son. Rockets should be launched. Sons should be loved. I know that now.

Most college application stories have happy endings. I hope, that by sharing mine, I can help other crazy parents enjoy happy beginnings and middles as well.

Acknowledgments

The following people have shared their stories, their friendship, and sometimes even their love with me, not only through the process of writing this book, but through the college application process as well. It wasn't pretty. I wholeheartedly thank the following people: Sharon Baronoff, Janice Blumberg, Linda Bowen, Gail Check, Nanci Ciarrocchi, Laura Szabo Cohen, Larry Dunsker, Victor Dye, Nancy Fine, Judy Gelade, Nancy Goldstein, Candace Helmsttetter, Anna Hoelscher, Lisa Kasdin Hyman, Edye Kamensky, Jeremy and Rakefet Kasdin, Phyllis and Albert Kasdin, Susan Klehr, Elayne Klein, Amy Levine, Laura Blake Peterson, Janet Poland, Ruthellen Rubin, JoAnn Sachs, Scott and Sharon Schwartz, Judy Seelig, Carol Weinstein, and Marilyn Weinstein.

To my sons Andrew and Zack, who are numbers two and three in only the chronological sense. Thank you for embracing neglect the way you did.

And to Harold, my husband and anchor, I love you eternally. One down, two to go!

—Karin Kasdin

Chapter 1
Bragging Rights

T he highlight of my mother's tenure as a parent occurred
during a routine stop at the corner gas station. None of
her children were with her. In fact, the three of us were all
newly formed grownups and out on our own in various states
of the country and of being. She no longer had need for her
road-weary, dilapidated, robin's-abdomen red Ford station
wagon with the wood on the sides. Yet, she stubbornly refused
to think about a new car that might clog up only part of the
driveway, rather than the whole thing, and chose instead to
sputter down the streets of Rochester, New York in an old
clunker she could well afford to discard.

That tank was her *nachesmobile*. *Naches*, as all Jewish children learn from the time they are applauded for their first firm
bowel movement, is a special kind of pride. *Naches* is a full
body swelling that parents experience when their child per-
forms a Chopin *Polonaise* to perfection or slam-dunks his way
onto the basketball travel team. *Naches* is also the by-product
of conceiving and raising a child who scores 1500 or better on
her SATs. In its purest form, *naches* is bragging rights—and my
mother had hers plastered on the rear window of her jalopy.

Watsamatta U:
A Get-a-Grip
Guide to
Staying Sane
Through Your
Child's College
Application
Process

The gas-pump jockey bit.

"Do you collect college stickers," he asked after spit-shining the rear window as Mom had requested, "or did you guys really attend all those schools?"

My mother is a large-breasted woman. Too much *naches* and she would never be able to keep her seatbelt fastened. With this question, she could feel it getting snug. How long she had waited for someone, *someone* to comment on her window, as precious to her as the Chagall stained glass windows at the Hadassah Hospital in Jerusalem, for which she had dedicated countless volunteer fundraising hours. She recited the statistics.

"My oldest daughter graduated from Northwestern and has a master's degree from Harvard. My middle daughter recently acquired her master's at the University of Rochester. With honors. My baby, the rocket scientist, is dotting the last few i's on his Ph.D. dissertation at Stanford. His bachelor's is from Princeton."

I think she thought the gas-pump jockey would drop dead from being more impressed than his non-college-educated self could handle. He didn't die, but flashed her a warm grin and said, "You must have done something right." Well, the home for retired station wagons could now scratch this red one from its waiting list indefinitely.

I am the daughter who graduated from Northwestern and Harvard and, trust me, neither venerable institution is profiling me in its marketing materials.

Don't get me wrong. I am very grateful to my parents and to the universities I attended for providing me with bountiful opportunities for personal and intellectual growth—a few of which I actually took advantage of when my social commitments didn't demand my full attention. Today I am leading a joyful life raising three of my own children and engaging in work that I love, thanks to the generosity of a husband with a sub-stantial income. (This is not a sexist arrangement; it is a selfish one. If I were a man, I'd be content to live off my wife's salary in order to pursue a life of letters.) I've never been offered a cabinet post. I've never even so much as exchanged a hello with Henry Kissinger. The Pulitzer Prize committee seems to have blacklist-ed me. I've window-shopped in the core of The Big Apple with-out one person stopping me for an autograph. I was too igno-rant to invest in Internet stocks when the investing was good.

The truth is, despite how much I value my years as a stu-dent in Chicago and Cambridge, I would probably be living the same life as I lead now if I had gone to Fred's College in Pick-Your-Nose, USA. (In fact, it would not have been a bad thing for me never to have discovered Chicago-style pizza.)

I am not a woman who regularly surprises herself. I am heavy into self-disclosure. I've had therapy. I am one with my neuroses. But I am dumbfounded that, when it came time for my firstborn son to apply to college, I found myself lusting after bragging rights. I coveted a prestigious sticker for my car. I ignored all of the remarkable talents as well as the very human-ity of my darling child as I focused on the fact that the lazy slug would not be applying to the highest-ranked schools according to the *U.S. News & World Report* annual college survey.

For months I looked at a boy with a B average and respectable SAT scores, who never got into any trouble, as a slacker. I could have made his life a living hell—and tried to, but he had the strength of character to ignore my harangues.

We await the results of the application process. My son, Dan, is going on with his life. Mine has virtually halted and I write this book to figure out why.

What It Is Like Now

Watsamatta U:
A Get-a-Grip
Guide to
Staying Sane
Through Your
Child's College
Application
Process

When my mother (no underachiever herself, being Phi Beta Kappa from Northwestern and the University of Rochester) graduated from college, not only was it unusual for a woman to hold a degree, it was not yet the norm for your average Joe to have one either. Hard-working parents, particularly immigrant parents who came to America bedecked in twine and burlap, had much to brag about when their offspring became educated. A college degree, come to find out, was not paid for by scooping pocketfuls of gold off the streets. Higher education fifty years ago said as much about the tenacity and work ethic of the parent as it did about the intellectual prowess of the child.

Today, millions of Doc Martens, Steve Maddens, and Nikes tread the hallowed halls of colleges and universities. Millions of dollars in financial aid are doled out to those who would otherwise be denied access to our institutions of higher learning due to having a net worth less than that of France. Still, there are families for whom college is either unattainable or not a priority. I know that many, many families are unable to send their children to school. But, from my privileged vantage point, in a relatively affluent suburb of a large Northeastern city, kids go to college—no questions asked.

Today, *naches* is no longer gleaned from simply having your child go to college. Now, the amount of *naches* you reap from the seeds you have sown is directly proportional to the *status* of your child's college or university.

Am I all wet? Do all parents who are not me *really not care* which school their children attend? If I am wrong, then explain to me why everyone I know spent more than $1000 on *The Princeton Review* for the SATs. Everyone I know doesn't have a spare thousand to throw away. Explain the proliferation of private schools and private tutors and private coaches and private therapists that we sic on our young people. What about the couple featured in *New York Magazine* who spent $500,000 annually on four tutors, an independent college counselor, two coaches, a physical therapist, a nutritionist, and a sports psychologist to ensure that their son, Deepak, would make it into Harvard? Deepak made it. *But so did the Unabomber, for God's sake!* Explain to me why Sylvan Learning Systems is a $300 million company currently trading at $13 per share and why Stanley Kaplan is important enough to be owned by *The Wall Street Journal.*

Well-intentioned parents like me are making a generation of children feel insecure at precisely the time in their lives when it should be our mission to make them believe they can conquer the world. I am writing this book on the chance it may help me discover why I'm behaving the way I am. My suspicion is that it will also help me discover why I and others think our children must "conquer the world" at all, instead of simply living in it.

Chapter 2

Our Trip Diary to College: Baby's First Breath

Our family's journey to college began the day after Dan was born.

Stubborn even in utero, Dan clung to my insides by his teeny tiny fingernails refusing to appear until he first put me through an exhausting twenty-four-hour labor, an excruciating and futile attempt at natural childbirth, and a Cesarean section finale. I was too fatigued to choose between breast or bottle, much less Princeton or Harvard, so I spent one whole glorious day in love with my son for who he was and not for whom he could become.

Twenty-four hours later, however, on a resplendent June day, that I knew about from the newspaper and not the dingy square of glass the hospital staff glibly called a window, I looked into my baby boy's hazel eyes and saw that someone really smart was nestled behind them. God help me—and him. It's true: most new mothers think their newborns are brilliant, but mine really was! My conclusion was further supported by the fact that Dan knew how to nurse instinctively. He taught *me* the fine points of nursing. Today, as a three-time veteran of motherhood, I am well aware that almost all babies nurse instinctively, but back then he was a sucking prodigy!

Dan's grandparents unanimously corroborated that he was indeed off the charts in cerebral development. None of them had prior grandparenting experience, but all of them are exceptionally bright people and certainly able to discern a superior mind inside a baby whose skull hadn't even completely closed yet.

At eight and a half months old, Dan walked. He looked like a little homunculus tooling around the house on feet the size of D batteries. Very few babies walk at eight months of age. I knew this because back then my folly was devouring parenting books. In my pre-"winging it" days, I actually thought that coaching from the experts could help me become a paragon of parental perfection who could instill in my child such things as the value of good nutrition. Ha! But back to walking ....

Because Dan walked so early, I felt confident that he would have an advantage over his peers in negotiating the ice-slicked streets of Cambridge or Princeton or New Haven when the time came. Eighteen years later, I observe that his brothers, neither of whom walked before their first birthdays, remarkably, are as skillful at walking as Dan. They walk in the same right-left-right-left pattern that he favors, and they don't usually fall down unless they are tripped.

My home regularly swells with teenagers. I take stock of them from an acceptable distance and note that, without exception, their gross motor skills are right on target. Obviously, the age at which young children reach their early milestones is inconsequential when trying to separate the academic wheat from the chaff. However, as brand new parents of a child we perceived as only slightly less exalted than the messiah himself, we felt an obligation to him and to the world to proactively jumpstart his cognitive development. We wanted

Watsamatta U:
A Get-a-Grip
Guide to
Staying Sane
Through Your
Child's College
Application
Process

to ensure his future high academic performance. Toward that end, we amassed a literary arsenal, believing that all good things come to one who reads.

Parenting experts and laypeople are united in their commitment to the written word, upon which all academic success hinges. "Read to your child," they collectively preach. "Read and read and read. When you read to your child consistently, you are planting seeds that will flower into a lifelong love of literature and learning."

This theory is so basic and sensible that you just want to shoot the guys who accumulate mountains of money from new parents, particularly young ones, willing to spend bucks they don't have for advice they don't need.

Still, sensible or not, I wonder … does the "read to your child and he will love reading" axiom apply to golf as well? "Play golf with your grownup consistently and she will develop a lifelong passion for golf?" I ask because I could watch someone play golf daily from March to January and not want to try golf. I could watch her stunning hunk of a pro who moonlights as a Calvin Klein underwear model wrap his muscular arms around her to demonstrate a stance and nip her ear in the process … and still not want to try golf. I could watch her squeal with ecstasy over a hole in one, then have the best sex of her life with her golf club and maybe even with the pro too … and *still* not want to try golf. I'd rather read.

I will never regret having read to my three sons. My babies provided me with excuses to peruse charming new works in children's literature I would never have discovered if childless. The hours I spent entwined with flannel-clad little bodies, tenderly reading as I breathed in the fleeting baby smells of Mr. Bubble and Cheerios, are jewels to me in memory now. Hundreds upon hundreds of evenings, for nearly ten years, I was steeped … first in Seuss and Scarry and later in E.B. White and A.A. Milne. Dan would suck the life out of his right thumb while I read to him, and with the left he would unconsciously twist his auburn curls into tight spirals. When he was sick, reading was a warm poultice. After suffering parental wrath or punishment, a hug and a book were needed guarantees that his world was shatter-free. What had its beginning as a mentally nutritious activity became a pure act of motherly love, unfettered by thoughts of college or future success. I read to my sons as much for my own tactile experience as for any intellectual benefits they would derive. And thank God!

In the early grades, if the fluent readers were the dolphins, Dan was a dolphin. Today, if the lovers of literature are the dolphins, he is definitely a flounder. Despite being a capable and fluent reader, the last book Dan picked up for pleasure was the owner's manual to his Volkswagen Jetta. All those hours we logged looking for Waldo were invaluable to him as he negotiated his way through the gaskets and spark plugs hidden in complex little car diagrams. He claims that he reads *Rolling Stone* magazine religiously. Frankly, I think he just worships at the altar of Jennifer Lopez—and not because he's a fan of her music. Dan takes pride in the fact that he hates reading, or at least he takes pride in the fact that he can get me all worked up when he claims that he hates reading.

I've suggested that extensive reading improves one's vocabulary, stretches one's mind, and flexes one's intellectual muscles. To paraphrase his response, which has grown more colorfully profane over the years, he functions perfectly well in society with the vocabulary he has already accrued. To Dan (and his brothers in turn), reading is what you do when you stink at sports. This, from a child who was selected by his English class to play Macbeth! As Shakespeare would put it, "There's the rub!"

Reading has always nourished my soul. At the beach I can devour nine books in a week. Reading keeps me from focusing

10

Watsamatta U:
A Get-a-Grip
Guide to
Staying Sane
Through Your
Child's College
Application
Process

on the sand in my butt. After my morning walk, my children watch me park myself in my blue and white chair with a delicious tome and linger there until the sun sinks over the horizon signifying guacamole time. They believe I read to assuage my feelings of inadequacy over not being able to surf. In the wintertime, they think I read because I can't ski. They are right that I can't ski and I can't surf. But if they think I don't know anything about either sport, they're wrong. I read.

The question is: Are my children the only healthy children on the planet to defy every educational principle espoused by Ed.D.s from Harvard to UCLA over the past twenty years? Are they the only living examples of the much less touted "Read to your child incessantly and he will be guaranteed to hate reading for the rest of his life" theorem? For my own sanity, I have to doubt it.

Back to my case study. Dan was not hailed as the second coming of Einstein in "the big boy school." School simply moved too slowly for him. He indicated his displeasure with the pace by regularly falling asleep at his desk, which caused his teacher to recommend that we consider either a remedial program or a second shot at first grade. I was baffled. He seemed so bright and inquisitive at home! A decade later, after having experienced three vastly different children and a gaggle of teachers ranging from inspirational to toxic in both the private and the public sectors, I have formulated two theories that address this paradox.

The first is polite and has to do with Dan. Having been weaned on *Sesame Street* and enriched by a stay-at-home mother obsessed with immersing her firstborn in educationally sound interactive play experiences, it would naturally take a little while for this particular youngster to adjust to a somewhat slower-paced academic environment where he would have to share front and center with twenty-five other equally talented and deserving children of obsessed parents.

My second, less polite theory has to do with school. I believe that the curricula of both our public and private schools have been designed to suck every shred of creativity and curiosity out of our children just in time for winter break of first grade. Teaching methods have not been updated since these children's parents were first required to memorize their multiplication tables. Four-year-olds today are deeply involved in interactive technologically advanced learning games. They play incessantly with computers and Game Boys that require them to develop sophisticated strategies for advancing in the game. Even kids with no benefit of computer technology watch *Sesame Street* and its clones. Years of painstaking research went into the development of these programs so that they might systematically shorten the attention span of several generations of Americans. (This, of course, is my opinion, even though I *still* love the show.)

Why am I doing the same homework in the same way with my seven-year-old as I did with Dan, who is now almost eighteen? The world is smaller, smarter, and wired from pole to pole now. I shouldn't be able to do my children's homework with them without first enrolling myself in some kind of crash course in techno-education for the new millennium.

Dan attended a Jewish Day School through third grade. He was on the receiving end of state-supervised secular curriculum for half the day and the study of Hebrew and religion for the other half day. Each month the programs were reversed so math, science, and social studies would not always be taught after lunch when attention spans were waning. We noticed an interesting pattern emerge the longer Dan stayed in this school. He excelled in Hebrew and all religious classes. He also managed to stay out of a coma in these classes, even when they were taught in the afternoons. However, his lackadaisical attitude persisted toward the portion of his education that colleges would actually evaluate when considering him for admission.

12

Watsamatta U:
A Get-a-Grip
Guide to
Staying Sane
Through Your
Child's College
Application
Process

We could deduce the reason simply by emptying out his Ninja Turtles book bag every evening.

In it, we'd find challah he had baked for the Sabbath and song lyrics he was learning for the next holiday celebration. The Hebrew language itself is a puzzle, with shapes and letters moving across the page from right to left, instead of the other way around, and sounds that emanate from the epiglottis and produce spit, unlike any sounds in the English language. He and his buddies learned Israeli dances in class and were regaled with stories about floods and oceans parting and a little boy who killed a giant with a slingshot.

And every night, stacked neatly in the pocket of his Ninja Turtles folder were dittos for the rest of his classes. Math dittos and social studies dittos and dittos that needed parental signatures and dittos announcing the commencement of new units of study requiring more dittos. Dan has always been a child who'd rather learn about Picasso by painting like him than by reading about him. I think most kids are with Dan.

Needless to say, in first grade, Dan was turning the school on with his smile, but not with his performance. (As an aside, *yes*, he has read this. Reading things about himself isn't anathema to him, as is reading about anything else. And his ego is strong enough to withstand his mother's lunatic ravings, provided he is assured that, in the final analysis, it is mom and not Dan who is portrayed as crazy. I, of course, promised him that this would be the case. Unfortunately, it also happens to be the truth.)

To my credit, I doggedly refused to deviate from Dan's educational plan. He would *not* be transferred to a remedial class. He would *not* require extra tutorials. He would absolutely, unequivocally, unquestionably *not* repeat first grade.

I was a pillar of stone.

"For God's sake," I cried, becoming the unyielding advocate that every parenting book demands you become for your child when you know in your bones what is right. "Don't you people recognize *boredom* when you see it? Try stimulating him and see what happens! Look up the word 'creativity'!"

My husband suggested that we might be in denial about Dan. I was *not* in denial. I was in *anger*. This was a child who could take apart the television and reassemble it as a toaster-oven!

So, he was moved up to second grade, where he could sleep on a whole new desk.

Dan's second-grade teacher (no, I am not going to deconstruct his education grade by grade) recognized the gleam in his eye that I had detected the moment they placed him in my baby-hungry arms. Dan sensed that she sensed the way his mind worked. Without fuss or calling attention to any "plan," they formed a mutual admiration society and Dan blossomed in her class in both secular and non-secular arenas. This established a twelve-year pattern in which Dan would excel in the classes taught by inspirational teachers and play possum in the classes taught by the duds.

Truly gifted teachers … teachers who love teaching and haven't been burned out by too many years of youthful exuberance or teenage angst … teachers who inject some spunk into a half-century old curriculum, who relate to their students individually because that is what they are *supposed* to do, who deep in their souls honestly want each of their students to succeed … are almost as extinct a species as the dot-com bazillionaire. They're still out there, but given the low status, measly income, and now the danger inherent in the teaching profession, it is unlikely that your child will enjoy more than one or two of these teachers in his educational lifetime.

Let's do the math. For the sake of easy computation, say your child will land in an inspirational teaching environment half the time. If your child's performance is directly proportional to the quality of the teaching as our son's was, he or she

14

Watsamatta U:
A Get-a-Grip
Guide to
Staying Sane
Through Your
Child's College
Application
Process

will exceed expectations half the time and disappoint you the other half. This usually averages out to a solid B. You most likely will not be purchasing any Harvard stickers for the back of your car and no UVA for the SUV. If your child, on the other hand, can overlook the deficiencies in even the most jaded of teachers and excel in a course that is taught by an android, then to the price of a college education add the price of a really good car. You may be driving it for decades because you can't take those stickers with you.

Who Is to Blame?

Loath as I am to admit it, my husband Harold may be somewhat right. I may have waded a teensy, tiny bit into the waters of denial once or twice over the past eighteen years. Although I am resolute in my belief that our educational system is in desperate need of updating and that inspiration from teachers translates to motivation in students, I am willing to admit that it would be a tad unfair to hold the schools solely responsible for the texture of Dan's personal transcript.

True it is that he is not onus-free. Millions and millions of young people before him, including his very own parents, were educated in the very same system. We all make choices. Some of us choose to play the game according to antiquated rules. Some of us make our own rules and build our own systems. Some of us drop out of all systems entirely. Dan made his choice. It was to work as diligently as he felt necessary in order to earn a respectable, but not necessarily frameable report card. Remember, I am not writing about a child who failed to complete his homework. I am writing about a child who failed to complete his homework *to my satisfaction*. Dan was churning out blintzes when I knew he could make Crepes Suzettes.

So what can you do with your frustration that would be more constructive than banging your head against a wall? I tried banging *his* head against the wall.

You can't very well punish a child for not living up to the potential you continue to believe lies within him when he is consistently completing everything that is expected of him. Even I knew that would be unjust. The only sensible tactic is to drown the child in loving support. I became the poster mom for loving support. In hot pursuit of the valedictorian I could see in my mind's eye, I took the following loving and supportive measures:

1. I bought him books. For roughly twelve years of gift-giving occasions, I would buy him something he wanted and also something *I* wanted him to have, which was always a book. I began by buying him the classics I thought every boy should love, such as *Treasure Island* and *Robinson Crusoe*. When those became coasters for Mountain Dew cans, I bought him books that had no appeal to me whatsoever, but that I dared to hope would spark a scintilla of interest. I bought Michael Jordan's biography, Jerry Seinfeld's book, and a fat book of slightly off-color cartoons. Last year I decided to collect the books and donate them to a charity, but they were as gone as gone could be. Some kid in Bora Bora could be reading them by now and laughing at the love notes I sketched in the inside covers.

2. I banned television. About two hundred times. I thought banning television would leave him with free time that, for lack of other options, he would fill with mind-expanding activities. He rearranged the furniture in his room four times, picked most of the paint off his window seat, and perfected an incredibly sophisticated and nuanced impersonation of bok choy.

3. I paid him to do well. Two bucks for each A. One for each B. Twenty bucks for a semester of mostly A's. A television in his room at the end of the year if he pulled straight A's. You can imagine how motivating this was. He said he had a better chance of winning the Pennsylvania State Lottery Jackpot *and* being struck by lightening on the way to collect it than of ever getting that TV in his room.

16

Watsamatta U:
A Get-a-Grip
Guide to
Staying Sane
Through Your
Child's College
Application
Process

4. When Dan was twelve years old, I sent him to a writing tutor who made him write essays about cats and other subjects of absolutely no interest to him. He took an instant disliking to her. My husband took an instant disliking to her fee. Dan's English grade remained constant, his petulance tripled, and we terminated.

5. I let friends talk me into believing that private school would be the answer to our prayers.

"There's nowhere to hide in private school," they claimed emphatically. "There's too much individualized attention happening there for a kid to get lost in the system."

How could I not have known that if you want to hide from individualized attention, all you have to do is slither silently behind your own eyeballs. Anyone is capable of being someplace and of not being there at the same time. Certainly a kid as bright as Dan has full mastery over that little trick.

"All the kids there go to the best colleges. He wouldn't want to be out of *that* loop."

"Of course he wouldn't," we thought. We withdrew Dan from a prestigious public school system that remunerates its teachers at top dollar and thus can recruit the best that the teaching profession has to offer, which means most teachers have master's degrees, and we enrolled him in a prestigious private school that pays its teachers wages you could amass simply by keeping your eyes on the sidewalk for a day or two and that results in hiring policies that require all new teachers to be out of college for at least one week.

During his three-year stint in private school, Dan did have a few excellent teachers, but not with the consistency that his friends had back in ye olde overcrowded public school. I know this to be true because his best friend lived with us for his entire junior year. I was able to assess Dan's education and Ed's—and I liked Ed's better. Granted, we live in an affluent suburb whose public school system is a stellar example of what the public schools can be. Many people who aren't in close proximity to this kind of school system can and do benefit from private schools. Dan's private school was a one-hour bus ride away. He hated the ride, missed his friends, and, to his credit, wanted to be part of a more diverse population. Had his grade point average soared in private school, we would have insisted that he complete his education there. But his GPA was carved in cement. We withdrew him and let him spend his senior year with his buds in his old school, having satisfied ourselves that some things aren't necessarily superior just because you pay for them.

6. When all attempts at controlling the uncontrollable failed, I chose a far easier and more organic means than loving support to try to get through to Dan. I tried relentless pestering—and found early on that I had a natural talent for it. I mercilessly pestered him as I clung by my obsessively manicured nails to delusions that pestering actually yields results.

My harangues of choice were as follows:

"It wouldn't hurt you to go above and beyond once in a while."

"Don't you see? If you devoted only five more minutes a day to homework, you'd have your choice of any college in the country."

"Turn off the goddamn TV, you lazy bum!"

"What do you mean you finished your homework in school? School is over at 2:30. You don't even open your eyes until three!"

"No, you may *not* go out. It's a school night. Do me a favor and at least *pretend* you care about your future."

"What did you get on the history test? A B? Why only a B? You have it in you to get an A. You didn't study enough."

18

Watsamatta U:
A Get-a-Grip
Guide to
Staying Sane
Through Your
Child's College
Application
Process

"What did you get on the math test? A B plus? Why only a B plus? You have it in you to get an A."

"What did you get on the science test? An A? So why didn't you get an A on the last one?"

"Maybe I should quiz you. Do you want me to quiz you? I think it will help if I quiz you. Why don't you want me to quiz you? Sit down, I'm quizzing you!"

(His personal favorite.) "Ed got an A on that test. Ed studied for hours for that test. Ed's going to get into any college he wants. Why can't you be more like Ed?"

Can you believe I'm admitting to this?

Some readers must be thinking by now that I am a true lunatic. Perhaps that is true, but I know that some of you are secretly relating to this. And I have met dozens of parents just like me. We are likeable. We have friends. We are highly functional in society. Right now I am certain that some equally misguided moms and dads are recognizing their own neurotic behavior in my confessional and we are right now bonding through the miracle of the written word.

I am taking no literary license when I say that my personal objectives for Dan took precedence over even my God-given maternal instincts to love him unconditionally. I do now and have always loved him unconditionally. It's the easiest thing I have ever done because he is quite simply a marvelous package of youthful exuberance, talent, remarkable resilience, and, most important, deep-down goodness.

Lucky for him to have been granted the brains and the ego to recognize a Screaming Mimi when he sees one and to go about his business despite the fact that she lives in his house. A lesser young man would have bolted years ago. Fortunately, Dan is also astute enough to recognize a blessed life when he's in one. Our relationship, unless I really am delusional, is solid. He has promised to have lunch with me four times before he leaves for college … a promise I extracted from him on a day he was particularly low on cash. I can still finagle a goodnight kiss, and once every month or so he submits to joining us for dinner. In sane moments, I know I escaped estrangement by the skin of my teeth. (Had my mother been the nag-meister I eventually became, my life would have been drastically different. Fiercely independent, I may have ended up in a teenage halfway house rather than endure it.)

Dan doesn't have to endure it. Far healthier than I, he chooses to ignore it. This is clearly illustrated by the fact that he will be graduating in four months—provided he successfully completes an extensive graduation project that he has yet to begin. It was assigned freshman year.

Ten Tips That Can Save You from Being Me During the Formative Years

1. You, the parent, cannot turn Johnny or Susie, the child, onto academic achievement merely by wishing. We all know that wishing, even really creative wishing where God gets involved, doesn't work all by itself. You must take action.

2. Taking action doesn't work either. No amount of nagging, pestering, tormenting, punishing, or quizzing will cause a kid to exert any more academic energy than he or she is compelled to exert. And yet, the experts continue to devise new and supposedly well-tested schemes for bettering the odds of producing an Ivy Leaguer. I read in the paper just yesterday that a desk and a good lamp can make all the difference to a child as he or she approaches the homework process. Give me a break, puh-lease! Granted, I am a mother and not an expert, but I postulate that a highly motivated student can produce awe-inspiring prize-worthy homework assignments on cinder blocks and plywood, while a disinclined child will use a state-of-the-art desk technologically outfitted for the new millennium as a repository for yesterday's underwear.

20

Watsamatta U:
A Get-a-Grip
Guide to
Staying Sane
Through Your
Child's College
Application
Process

These are the very same experts who purport that with patience you can get your child to choose to eat nutritionally. Ha! We all know that you can place a meal in front of your child that looks like a photo in *You Are a Model Parent Magazine,* but no one has yet invented a non-invasive prod that will unlock a clenched jaw and then chew the food and swallow it without your child being aware of it. If you can't get your child to eat what you deem nutritious, you certainly won't be able to beg, cajole, or manipulate him into performing well in school if he doesn't want to, no matter how much happy homework assistance you provide.

3. A perfectly pleasant Ozzie-and-Harriet-style evening can disintegrate into a scene from *Who's Afraid of Virginia Woolf?* at the mere mention of homework. Give it up.

4. Giving it up requires *really, really* giving it up in the deepest part of your most neurotic place—and also knowing exactly what "it" is that you are giving up. You are giving up some very basic and deeply rooted beliefs.

Our limited imaginations have led us to believe that our chance for success and happiness in adult life is entwined into a web we begin to weave while we're still in Pampers. The high school valedictorian will always be accepted into the college of her choice whose alumni form nationwide networks of highly skilled and highly compensated professionals who will later offer financial security through a flextime job as Chief of Everything that allows for plenty of quality parenting time composed of hours of happy homework assistance so baby can follow in Mom's path and become equally successful and worry-free.

Or the flip side ...

If Billy gets one more detention he will be suspended from school just like his dad was twenty-five years ago. Billy's dad is a complete failure and an embarrassment to the family. He's lost twelve jobs in eight years and is currently selling vegetable peel art on the streets of Utica, New York. He also perpetually sings *Kumbaya* to himself and urinates directly into sewers to eliminate "the middle man." Everyone in town knows that Billy's dad never completed his homework with regularity. And everyone fears a similar fate for everyone's own child if yesterday's book report isn't handed in until tomorrow.

I hope I can relinquish ludicrous and useless fictional scenarios such as these in time to save my next two children from my past self. I was lucky enough to have my first child first. I don't think either of the other two could or would put up with the nonsense I managed to dredge up especially for Dan. Plus, all that happens when you try to change the inherent nature of your children is that you age really quickly from all the stress. I spent years planning on basking in my children's reflected glory. But as can happen when you worship the sun, the pursuit of reflected glory too can cause permanent wrinkles. Frankly, I'm exhausted.

5. Remember: If your child learns how to love, you have been an inspirational parent and teacher.

6. Remember: If your child is kind to others, he has achieved greatness.

7. If our definition of success is Harvard, more than 99% of our children are failures.

8. Know that when you wished for the perfect child, your wish was granted.

9. Do you always work as hard as you could? *Well, why not?* Do any of us really know who is working up to his potential and who isn't? Maybe Einstein's potential far exceeded his accomplishments. Maybe he had the potential to discover a force that would make love, not war.

10. Try to limit yourself to one ice cream per day.

Chapter 3

Enough Background Already. What About College?

The First College Seminar

All the years of fighting and fantasizing aside, the actual nuts-and-bolts process of choosing a college or having a college choose you officially begins in the second half of your child's junior year when Mr. Admissions Director from the U of XYZ comes to school on a Wednesday evening to present a seminar called "Getting the Facts About Getting into College" or "The College Connection" or something similar. Unfortunately, our junior and his girlfriend broke up the afternoon before the evening of our college seminar. Consequently, he left his insides at home and only his pod accompanied us to the event. Dan could barely keep his head up off the table, much less listen attentively and fill out forms.

If I had been the good mother I profess to be, I would have used that evening to console my son over his severed relationship. This had been his first serious girlfriend. I should have soothed his bruised ego by telling him that she was a bitch who never deserved him in the first place. I should have mollified him by assuring him that there are several girls in places yet unknown to him, whom he has yet to meet and yet to love, and that his misery will abate with time, and surprisingly little of it at that. I should have told him about the remarkable curative power of time. I should have held him close to me and shared the wisdom we all accrue through our own broken hearts. But unfortunately, the other thing about time is that it waits for no one and we had to get our rears in gear if we wanted to nab the good seats. Time doesn't heal the information gap when you miss your first college seminar night.

Truthfully, Dan may or may not have shared his emotional burden with me that evening. It's a fifty-fifty shot on ordinary days when nothing competes for our time and attention. Had he been inclined to let me mother him that evening, though, I callously, albeit not consciously, let that far too rare chance to nurture his soul slip away from me forever and I am forever the poorer for it.

I didn't feel warm and fuzzy toward Dan on that cold, February evening. On that cold, February evening I was almost unendurably embarrassed by my son's visible lack of interest. I wanted to bludgeon him as he slept on the cafeteria table. I leaned over to whisper in my friend's ear that Dan was skating on very thin ice and, as I did, I noticed that her daughter *wasn't even there!* Apparently she had a major exam the next day for which she hadn't begun to study, even though she knew about both the exam and the college seminar night more than three weeks ahead of time. She stayed home to cram and sent Mom and Dad as her emissaries. She had every confidence that they would hang on every word uttered by Mr. Admissions Director and parrot each one back to her in the same order in which he had spoken them.

I scanned the audience. The Lonely Hearts Club must have been in the midst of a membership drive that night. Could it possibly be that every boy there had either dumped or been dumped by his girlfriend that afternoon? Heads were dropping

24

Watsamatta U:
A Get-a-Grip
Guide to
Staying Sane
Through Your
Child's College
Application
Process

onto tables in synchronicity. Eyelids were drooping as though someone had painted the ceiling with pollen. The atmosphere became thick with the air from a hundred stifled yawns. A few of the girls seemed moderately interested in what Mr. Admissions Director had to say. At least their eyes were open. One of them—the valedictorian, I suppose—took notes.

Cut to the parents. Rapt. Unblinking. Trying their best to absorb new information as they mentally tallied the plusses and minuses of their own children and measured them against the attributes this man ascribed to a solid college admissions candidate. I took another look at my son the lox and put a minus sign in the column for "able to hold up own head." It was going to be a long evening.

We were shown several real college applications that had been submitted to Mr. Admissions Director the year before. One stands out in my mind. It was an eight-page, four-color brochure that looked like the annual report that comes to me in the mail once a year from the Walt Disney Company because my son was given a few shares as a Bar Mitzvah gift. The hopeful candidate's freckled face graced the cover of the brochure. Inside were pictures of him booting a soccer ball, hammering a nail for Habitat for Humanity, playing the guitar for his friends, and meditating upon the natural beauty of a windblown wheat sheaf in a sun-bleached field. And speaking of Bar Mitzvahs, this could have made a great favor, certainly one Aunt Rivka would have cherished forever.

The brochure listed, in various complementary ink colors, the young man's accomplishments in the athletic, academic, and personal arenas. On the back cover were a short poem and the boy's Web site address.

I prayed that we would be told how ludicrous and unnecessary this monumental and expensive effort in salesmanship was, and we were told exactly that. I silently congratulated myself for forgetting to bring the camera to any events that weren't celebrated with cake. This boy's parents either had no confidence in their son's ability to let his credentials speak for themselves or else they had huge stockpiles of money crying out to be burned. It goes without saying that this student was not admitted to the U of XYZ. Apparently, his credentials did not look nearly as impressive in black and white.

We were shown another applicant's creation ... a complex series of graphs delineating the student's participation in extracurricular activities according to the hours spent in each. A line graph indicated a nice upswing in involvement from the ninth grade to the twelfth. This is a good thing. You don't want to see a child repeatedly dropping out of activities or becoming a slug senior year. On the other hand, if this child's painstakingly created graphs were accurate, she would have accomplished what most time-squeezed, overworked Americans only yearn to achieve—she would actually have fit twenty-seven hours into a twenty-four-hour day. According to her statistics, she spent more time in extracurricular activities than she spent breathing. She too was rejected—or, rather, not admitted to the U of XYZ.

(I've learned through my research that colleges never *reject* applicants. They simply decline to admit them. The word "reject" apparently wreaks havoc on the adolescent ego. I suspect, though, that semantics don't go very far toward cushioning the blow of not gaining entrance to the school of your dreams. I rarely hear kids tell their friends that they have been "denied admission" to Suchandsuch University. The kids themselves don't tap dance around the vocabulary.)

That evening was the first of many times during the next half year that we would hear laudatory spiels about the humanity of the college admissions staff. Mr. Admissions Director told us that, while he can't speak for admissions departments nationwide, he was proud to lead a group of men and women who took their jobs very seriously, who were truly committed not only to the

Watsamatta U:
A Get-a-Grip
Guide to
Staying Sane
Through Your
Child's College
Application
Process

university, but to each and every one of the 40,000 applicants whose futures they held in their compassionate hands.

In our travels since that evening, and through my extensive reading of books written by and about college admissions departments, I feel that I *can* speak for admissions personnel nationwide. I have learned that *all* admissions officers are cut from the same cloth. They *all*:

◆ took this job in the first place because they feel most at home in an academic environment and desperately want your child and all children to matriculate at a college where their individual strengths and talents are recognized and appreciated.

◆ remember what it felt like to be on the receiving end of a college admissions decision. (This is not difficult to believe, as most of the admissions people we met were about twenty-two years old and thus on the receiving end a mere four or five years ago. See chapter on *The Interview*.)

◆ are the nicest group of people you'd ever want to meet.

◆ are people with whom you would like to go on a canoe trip or other outdoor adventure.

◆ are willing to log countless hours to ensure that every application is given a thorough and careful evaluation.

◆ try not to read applications when they are tired or not in the mood.

◆ despite never meeting your child, will look at her as a whole package rather than as a numerical representation of a person.

◆ never tested well either.

◆ performed just dandily in college, despite the aforementioned testing problem.

◆ made the most of their college years, despite having been "denied admission" to their first-choice schools.

- found out quickly that the college they attended should have been their first choice school, because it turned out to be a perfect match for them.

- regard the institution they represent as one of the most caring, people-oriented institutions in the country.

- review all applications with an eye toward admitting, not denying admission.

- sincerely care about your child's future.

Hearing that my child's application would be lovingly reviewed by strangers who truly have his best interests at heart, somehow failed to take the edge off the process for me. Call me a cynic.

We were shown a few more examples of what not to do ... videotapes of school plays, home-made television commercials marketing student flesh, essays obviously written by professional essayists, and essays with errors that scream at you, such as the apparently popular phrase, "I was recently abducted into the National Honor Society."

Finally, the session was opened for questions and answers. This is the portion of the evening when overexcited parents seize the opportunity to ask questions, the answers to which have already been explained in three or four different ways.

"So, what you're saying, then, is that written, visual, or three-dimensional supplements to the application do not necessarily improve a kid's chances of admittance," one mother asked as if she had been busy suffering a minor stroke during the half hour that this poor man devoted to just this very issue.

Please forgive the overused cliché, but *I hate when that happens!* She continued, "... because my son's grades aren't really impressive, but he creates museum-quality sculptures and furniture out of wood..."

28

Watsamatta U:
A Get-a-Grip
Guide to
Staying Sane
Through Your
Child's College
Application
Process

Mr. College Admissions Director cut her off at the pass. "Please don't send us a chair ... Shaker or Queen Anne or any other kind either. We sent the last three back!"

He began to look a little peaked. Mr. Woodworking Prodigy began to look suicidal.

"Just tell your son to write 'woodworking' down in the 'hobbies' box on the application, along with a brief—a very brief—sentence or two about his passion for the craft, and that will suffice."

Chairs apparently don't fall into the same category as shoes. A journalist from The New York Times recently spent some time in the admissions office of a prestigious university. One day a package arrived along with the daily intake of two hundred applications. When the admissions officer assigned to the case tore open the wrapping, he found a very decorative woman's shoe along with a note that said, "Now that I have one foot in the door, I hope you will consider my application carefully and admit the rest of me."

Despite this being an old, worn out job-hunting trick, the admissions office, the journalist, and even the venerable New York Times ate it up! Enough anyway, to give the story column space that I've been trying to obtain the old-fashioned way for decades! The powers that be at the university were quoted as saying that, while this display of ingenuity may not in itself be enough to gain admittance, it is surely enough to merit a very careful look at the rest of the application in the hope that it will be likewise impressive. I shudder to think what will be coming up over the transom next season. Jockey shorts, perhaps, in order to "jockey" for a spot in the freshman class?

Every year before Back to School Night, the principals of elementary, junior high, and high schools send home a directive admonishing parents not to use this forum as an opportunity to ask the teacher for information about their children.

"Teachers are happy to schedule conferences at a mutually convenient time," the letter says. "Back to School Night is a time to learn about our curriculum and programs."

Come on. Few parents care a whit about when Billy or Joey or Susie will begin the unit on dinosaurs. What they really want to know is ...

"Do you like my Billy or Joey or Susie?"

"Have you discovered that Billy or Joey or Susie is perfect yet?"

"Is Billy or Joey or Susie succeeding in your class?"

"Are you worthy of teaching my Billy or Joey or Susie?"

"Has Billy or Joey or Susie managed to keep his or her unfortunate habit of biting other children in check so far?"

A million or more anxious parents practically bite off their tongues in restraint on Back to School Night.

Not so on college seminar night. Parents acknowledge no boundaries that night. Thinking that this may be their one shot at getting the straight dope on their child, they fire statistics like Beebees and expect instant prognostications about their child's future to be fired back in return.

"My son has a 3.65 GPA and, while the SATs aren't until next week, he pulled a 1350 on his PSATs. Is it reasonable for us to apply to Stanford?"

When Dan began to snore loudly enough to call attention to himself, we felt it was reasonable to exit the premises. We were not the first to depart.

When the three of us were alone in the car, I decided that—as a personal protest—I would have Dan submit his application the old-fashioned way ... on paper, in ink, written by himself, with no accompanying documents or shoes or chairs, even though he does list woodworking among his hobbies.

Watsamatta U:
A Get-a-Grip
Guide to
Staying Sane
Through Your
Child's College
Application
Process

Dan regained both consciousness and hunger about twenty yards beyond school property. Never ones to deny him a cheese steak at the slightest mention that he craved one, we pulled into his favorite greasy spoon and grabbed a booth.

"The program was useless and the man was a geek," said Dan nonchalantly.

Thus began the first substantive college discussion we ever had with our son. It went something like this:

Chapter 4

Our First College Conversation: A Reenactment

Dan

(*taking a humongous bite of cheese steak*) I'm going to Duke.

Mom

I'm having Harrison Ford's baby. What's new with you, Harold?

Dad

I'm the only sane one among us. That's what's new. Why Duke?

Dan

They have an awesome basketball team.

Mom

That's nice, honey. You don't play basketball.

Dan

I *watch* basketball. I watch *a lot* of basketball. I watch *a lot* of *Duke* basketball.

Mom

Which is why you don't have the grades to get into Duke.

Dan

I have darn good grades.

32

Watsamatta U:
A Get-a-Grip
Guide to
Staying Sane
Through Your
Child's College
Application
Process

Mom

You have B's.

Dan

And your point is ...?

Mom and Dad

Duke wants A's.

Dan

Duke isn't even Ivy League.

Mom

A technicality. Duke is as difficult to get into as any Ivy League School ... and more competitive than some because the weather is warmer there.

Dan

That's the other plus. I'm sick of freezing my ass off in Pennsylvania in the winter. North Carolina would be a nice break.

Mom

I just don't think Duke is the right match for ...

Dan

You don't have any confidence in me. Dad, she doesn't have any confidence in me.

Mom

(Switching mood selector from incredulous to loving, supportive mode) I have all the confidence in the world in you, honey. There is not a shred of doubt in my mind that you will be accepted into an excellent college, succeed there, and then go on to make an indelible mark on the world. You are a very unique and intelligent young man with so much to offer in life.

Dan

I'm not talking about *life*. I'm talking about *Duke*. You don't have any confidence that I can get into Duke.

Mom

Well, you're right about that.

Dan

Mom, you are forgetting about something I have that no other kid has.

Mom

What's that?

Dan

(*Executing a simple, oft-used shrugging gesture with hands, accompanied by a killer smile*) I'm Dan!

Dad

He's Dan.

Mom

True indeed. However, last I checked, "Dan-ness" was not listed as one of the qualities colleges are looking for in their applicants. I just bought the *College Handbook 2001* published by The College Board. Let's just look up Duke and see if the listing mentions anything about Dan-ness.

Dan

I can live without your sarcasm, thank you very much.

Mom

My darling child, I am not trying to discourage you ...

Dad

Yes, you are. You are doing your damnedest to discourage him. You are going to discourage him from talking to you about this ever again. If the kid wants to apply to Duke, let him apply to Duke. It's $35 and then we'll know.

Dan

Thanks, Dad. When can we go visit?

Dad

The day after you get in. And, my friend, I strongly suggest you come up with some additional and more realistic choices.

34

Watsamatta U:
A Get-a-Grip
Guide to
Staying Sane
Through Your
Child's College
Application
Process

Dan

I'm way ahead of you. I want to look at a bunch of schools in the Boston area.

Mom

Boston. You should be nice and toasty up there.

Dad

Karin ...

Mom

I love Boston! I went to graduate school in Boston. I was hoping you'd say Boston. Let's go home and pull out the *College Handbook 2001* published by The College Board and look at some schools in Boston. And other places too. OK, sweetie? OK? This is going to be a wonderful adventure for us.

Dan

Not tonight. I've got a splitting headache.

This would be the first of several mutual Advil experiences.

Ten Tips for How to Have a Swell Time at College Night

1. Leave your child at home

2. If you bring your child, leave your expectations of his behavior at home.

3. Recognize that your child has no interest in college yet. The junior prom hasn't even taken place yet. Her focus right now is on the dress.

4. Facing an uncertain future can be terrifying. Terror is best dealt with through avoidance. Avoidance is best accomplished through sleep.

5. If you talk too much or ask too many redundant questions, there is a possibility that some other parent may wait for you in the parking lot with a pickax. It may be me.

6. Don't mention your child's 3.94 grade point average, even casually. The rest of the parents with average kids will telekinetically spit at you.

7. Wear your reading glasses. There are graphs.

8. Don't embarrass yourself or your child by talking to anyone under 40. Even if you listen to Bob Marley or drive a motorcycle, you are still not cool.

9. Don't talk to anyone over 40 either. The temptation is too great to compare notes on your kids.

10. Bring ice cream money.

Chapter 5

The College Handbook

The *College Handbook 2001*, published by The College Board, weighs four and three quarters pounds. "Handbook" is a misnomer. This compilation of exhaustive research definitely requires two hands to lift. Most of you have probably purchased it by now, so you know it's 1623 pages long. That's about a thousand pages more than my son has read in his lifetime. As I plunked down the $25.95, I didn't harbor any illusions about who would be combing through this invaluable information ... and all by myself.

I'm not sure why I selected this tome from among the dozens that line two or three bookcases at our local Barnes & Noble. The college guidebook industry is certainly enjoying robust health. Meticulous parents—and, trust me, parents are the *only* people you see in this aisle of the store—could spend the better part of a day and get a decent biceps workout as well, making fine discernments among guidebooks while their teenagers try out the new CDs or sip latte in the café.

Some books have catchier titles than the *College Handbook 2001*. Perhaps I chose this one because of the smiling faces of the well-scrubbed, gleeful, multiracial, American coeds The College Board employs as cover models. Of course, you don't know which of these sunshiny kids were admitted to the college of their choice, who made do with a safety school, or who, in fact, are not kids at all, but professional, grownup models who attended The College of Looking Really Young for Your Age. No matter. Luminous faces sell colleges. Or at least they sell books and catalogs that sell colleges.

Dan suffered the world's longest convenience headache because weeks went by before he was willing to spend five minutes with me and "the book," as it was nicknamed by our entire household. By the time he deemed himself physically capable of dealing with this incendiary subject, I had logged several hundred highly stressful hours poring over "the book's" content. It takes days just to wind your way through the forty (I kid you not!) indexes.

The forty indexes (I always thought the plural was "indices," but the book uses the word "indexes" in big letters on the front cover and The College Board should know these things!) are included for a reason. They exist to enable you to make the most effective use of the book. For example, how would I ever have found the Cincinnati College of Mortuary Science without an index?

You can search for a college by geographical location (which, I've already explained, makes no sense for me because my son wants to go to Boston but at the same time stay warm) or you can search by program, size, selectivity, student life, sports, SAT or ACT requirements, gender restrictions, and (of course) alphabetically. I did none of the above. I used the book for the singular purpose of looking up the profiles of colleges I was already considering for my son.

Having survived this process myself a mere twenty-seven years ago, I felt I knew what was out there. I am certain there

38

Watsamatta U:
A Get-a-Grip
Guide to
Staying Sane
Through Your
Child's College
Application
Process

exist fine institutions of higher learning to which I have never been exposed, that would fit Dan like a glove. Forget those colleges! Who wants to send a kid to a college no one's ever heard of? That sticker means nothing to gas station attendants or anyone else. When your hairdresser asks you where your son is going to college, the last response you want to hear when you tell her is "Where's that?" To my mind at the time, a mediocre school with a familiar name was preferable to a lesser-known college that might aspire to higher standards of excellence.

I read about Duke, of course, and they indeed are heavy into basketball. I was sure Dan's application would become a foul shot right into the wastebasket. I also read about UNC at Chapel Hill as well as numerous other large, competitive state schools. I scoured the Massachusetts pages, eliminating for religious reasons any school that was called Saint Somebody's, as well as all women's colleges, music conservatories, agricultural or technical schools, Harvard, and MIT. I compiled a nice little list of possibilities.

I also pored over descriptions of competitive but not ruthless colleges in the Northeast and the Midwest sectors. However, I don't want him exposed to places like California from which he might never return.

The profiles provide you with the following information:

Name of school (duh)

Location

Size

Private or Public

Percentage of Applicants Admitted

Deadlines

SAT or ACT Requirements

Cost

You'd think it would be impossible to memorize all of this information for one school, much less several. Well, I went to college. For me it only took a couple hundred readings to commit to memory a full fifty profiles without mixing up any of the data. I became a human microchip responding to the most casual of remarks with God knows how many megabytes of information.

"We're going to a convention in Ann Arbor this weekend," a friend explained as she declined my invitation to dinner.

"Ann Arbor," I replied. "Home to the University of Michigan. Public university. 24,000 undergraduates. $29,000 per year out-of-state. 560-660 verbal. 600-700 math. 89% of freshmen ranked in the top quarter of their high school class. Division 1 sports. Contact Theodore Spencer."

It has recently come to my attention that my brain must have disposed of old, dated information in order to make room for this new, timely knowledge. Last week I forgot that you must turn the oven on if you want the food inside of it to cook. I also seem to have forgotten that good dental hygiene can stave off oral surgery in one's golden years, because lately I have been neglecting to pack my toothbrush when I travel. This slip-up is particularly annoying when you arrive at your destination after the drugstores and hotel shops have closed, which I did just last

40

Watsamatta U:
A Get-a-Grip
Guide to
Staying Sane
Through Your
Child's College
Application
Process

week when I arrived at a cousin's wedding in Cleveland, Ohio, home to Case Western Reserve University, a small, private institution of 7,000 undergraduates. $25,600 total cost. 580-690 verbal. 620-720 math. 66% of freshmen ranked in top tenth of their high school class. Contact William T. Conley.

It's not funny. I would spew data at Dan at totally inappropriate times, such as when he was in a good mood. I'd wield it as a weapon when I felt he wasn't studying hard enough.

"89% of Boston University freshmen ranked in the top quarter of their high school class. You are road kill if you don't ace this upcoming math test. Why aren't you in your room studying?"

"I know the stuff, mom. And by the way, I *am* in the top quarter of my class."

"Oh. Then you can aspire to Tufts, where 75% of freshmen were in the top tenth."

You learn in Basic Child Psychology 101 that harping at your child does not go very far toward advancing your personal goals for that child. I took Child Psychology 101 *and* 102. I received A's in both. Why couldn't I stop myself from harping and simply leave the poor child alone? In the most buried, but enlightened pinpoint of a spot in my soul, I was painfully aware that I was in imminent danger of wreaking permanent damage on a relationship I had spent the major portion of my adult life nurturing. Dan was preparing to leave me and he would do so on either his terms or mine. If he left on his terms, a strong possibility would exist for us to establish a loving and mature relationship in the years to come. On my terms, I would get what I wanted, but only temporarily. As surely as I knew how to spell Rensselaer Polytechnic Institute, I knew that my continued uninvited interference would spell disaster.

I remember lying in my bathtub evening after evening and resolving again and again to let Dan take the lead in the college process. The worst that would happen, I told myself, would be that he would procrastinate and have to work for a year before matriculating. And this was only April of his junior year! I prayed for guidance. I enrolled in a class on Kaballah in order to find my own spirituality.

I tried backing off. It was a feeble attempt. Next month were the SATs and I had to see to it that he was well-prepared. I would back off big time once that hurdle had been surmounted.

Note: As I write this, all of Dan's applications have been completed and mailed. We have only to wait for the responses. As far as I know, he has never so much as glanced in passing at the *College Handbook 2001* published by The College Board. An unscientifically conducted survey I took leads me to conclude that neither have any of his friends … and Dan has a lot of friends.

Chapter 6

The Scholastic Aptitude Test (SAT)

S wathed in mystery for me since the day I first clutched my No. 2 pencil in dread and began to fill in the little circles that spelled my name, the SAT can cavalierly rupture the fragile self-esteem bubble of even a truly bright kid. It certainly blew *my* cover.

I was a conscientious student and attained the grades to prove it. It should come as no surprise, given the neuroses I have already laid bare in this book, that I was the kid who handed in the report a week *before* it was due. I would stay up nights gazing blankly into the eyes of the 237 Paul McCartneys I had stapled to my lavender bedroom wall and worry about whether I remembered to number my pages or punctuate my footnotes. I don't know if I overachieved because overachieving is in my DNA, or because I was terrified of repercussions from my parents if I slacked off, or because my social life consumed only four minutes a week, or because we only had three television channels and I had nothing better to do with my time than drool over Paul McCartney and memorize textbooks. Truthfully, I would much rather have passed the time as so many of my peers did, by getting high and singing Bob

Dylan songs and partaking of the sexual revolution. It would not be until college that I acquired the strength of character I needed to conform to the crowd.

But I digress. Suffice it to say, I meticulously crafted an image of myself as a scholar. This image was further enhanced when I became editor of the school newspaper, a totally ungroovy thing to do in 1971 because it wasn't even an underground paper.

Everyone expected me to catapult myself into the intelligentsia with my scores, but I knew from past demoralizing testing experiences that if I ever made it into *Who's Who,* I would not be listing my SAT scores among my proudest accomplishments.

I was right. I simply do not test well and, as of May 1972, I had the statistics to prove it. For the record, my verbal score indicated that I needn't be totally ashamed to call myself a writer, but my math score could have been achieved by a slug slinking his way across the calculator. Fortunately, in my adult life I can count exactly zero people who have asked me what I scored on my SATs. No one has ever brought it up, except for one guy I know who nonchalantly threw his perfect score into a dinner conversation once—but he's a horse's patoot so that doesn't count.

I don't remember being advised to take the SAT test repeatedly to improve my score. I don't remember anyone suggesting that a class or expensive private tutoring would be a wise move. I also have no recollection of my guidance counselor or any of my college interviewers telling me not to apply to the college of my choice because of my average showing on the SAT. I was admitted to the college of my choice *despite* my SAT scores. I worked diligently in college, graduated with honors, took the Graduate Record Examinations, performed miserably on them, and was admitted to *Harvard—for crying out loud!* In today's climate, Hahvahd would hah-hah me right out the door.

44

Watsamatta U:
A Get-a-Grip
Guide to
Staying Sane
Through Your
Child's College
Application
Process

We are in an SAT frenzy—and it doesn't speak to the best that human nature has to offer. According to the same *New York Magazine* article that introduced me to Deepak and his parents' half-million-dollar personnel bill, students with scores in the *1500s* are calling private tutors in tears and hysterically begging to pay fees of up to $400 per hour in order to achieve the elusive perfect score. No, I didn't get that number wrong. A friend of mine in Westport, Connecticut actually knows people who spend that!

Have we all gone mad?

Colleges no longer comfort us by saying that the SATs are only one indicator of a student's potential success in college, … that they look at the *whole person very carefully.* Instead, these days they print their required SAT scores in the college guides. At their information sessions they tell you exactly what scores they seek from prospective students. If asked outright, many of the more competitive schools will tell you that your child's numbers don't pass muster. Applications at some large, competitive state universities are run through computers before a human ever looks at them. If your child's SAT scores are below their cutoff, no one may even notice that she speaks seven languages or negotiated a hostage crisis in Rio. It's all very discouraging.

Let's say your child—not mine but yours—holds a laudatory 3.8 average from a distinguished public or private school, but has very unimpressive SAT scores. Red flag! While he is clearly an overachiever, which is good, college admissions people wonder whether or not he will be able to compete at very high academic levels or if at some point, due to his below-par aptitude, he will hit a wall and not have the innate capabilities to hold his own in a rigorous program.

Now, let's say your child has a 2.8 average, but SAT scores worth disseminating via the family holiday card. *Great big red flag!* He clearly doesn't work up to his potential, which does not bode well for his academic future.

We all want our kids to have high GPAs *and* high SAT scores. We also all want to get thin on the stromboli and cinnamon bun diet. The difference is, on that diet you can be guaranteed never to fit into your pants, but your child can, even with mediocre scores, fit into college. Bear in mind that there *really is* a college for everyone. Even kids with low-end SAT scores and mediocre grades get the hell out of the house and go to school.

Dan pulled average scores the first time he took the SAT, which planted his score solidly in the "not embarrassing" range, but significantly below the "wait-till-your-sick-grandfather-hears-this-it-will-give-him-a-reason-to-live" cutoff.

I had a slightly above average conniption.

"Of course you'll take them over," I said. "No question about it."

And of course I registered him for the *Princeton Review* crash course in SAT preparation. I didn't really *need* to see Greece this year anyway. The *Princeton Review* currently costs $799 for a class or, if your child is the president of student council *and* the lead in *Guys and Dolls,* making it impossible for her to squeeze into a class at the times it's offered, your alternative is to pay $100 an hour for a minimum of 10 hours but more realistically 15 to 20 hours, for a private tutor to come to your home at odd times, such as really late at night or really early Sunday morning—which is when I scheduled Dan's sessions.

First thing Sunday morning my son is flotsam. He uses this time to catch up on the sleep he missed by waking up early for school, competing in tennis tournaments both for school and for USTA, working part time, and, of course,

46

Watsamatta U:
A Get-a-Grip
Guide to
Staying Sane
Through Your
Child's College
Application
Process

socializing. Fortunately for my little boy, he can not only walk and chew gum at the same time, he can also prepare for the SATs in his sleep. Or he thought he could.

Upon reflection, I don't think it's a good idea to prepare for the SATs in the comfort of your own home … on the sofa … barefoot … in the sweatpants and T-shirt you slept in. Somehow the gravity of the endeavor is compromised. When you spend close to two grand on your uphill battle, you'd sort of like the soldiers to be properly attired. For all the dignity of the occasion, these hapless tutors could have been coming over to watch *Ally McBeal*.

Dan yawned and *shmoozed* his way through his sessions. The tutors (one for verbal, one for math) were impressed by his sweet nature, his sense of humor, and his personal style—none of which are measured by an SAT. He did dutifully perform the exercises and once or twice even completed the homework. At his final session, they assured me that we could expect to see at least a 100-point increase over his paltry showing on his first crack at it. That is what the *Princeton Review* guarantees … 100 points higher than your "untutored" test or you win free extra sessions. Can you beat that? 100 points for $800 if you take a class. 100 points for $2,000 if you get house calls.

Liberal by both birth and choice, my heart broke for the millions of students nationwide who, due to economic circumstances over which they have no control, must face their SATs unassisted. This group included several of Dan's friends. Like the television commercials for I forget which mid-range car that ask, "Do only rich people deserve a spacious interior?" I've asked myself numerous times, "Do only rich kids deserve an extra hundred points on their SATs?"

The SATs were, I believe, designed to measure aptitude. Today they measure a student's ability to cram for what was once billed as an uncrammable test. I wish I could believe that people with money are only deluding themselves when they think that these test preparation programs work. I wish someone would show me statistics clearly indicating that students who take a few sample tests on their own perform as well as their tutored peers. But if this were true, why the proliferation of supplemental study programs? These programs must enjoy some degree of success. I deplore the system and I berate myself regularly for having bought into it.

The tutors, who were both young, attractive women in their mid-20s—no small distraction for a hormonally driven seventeen-year-old—told us they didn't know what to hope for. If Dan failed to collect on his extra hundred points, they'd have the pleasure of returning to see him. That's my boy!

It wasn't *Dan's* fault that the SAT exam was administered the morning after the Friday night that *Star Wars: The Phantom Menace* opened. It wasn't *his* fault that the only tickets left by the time his posse reached the box office were for the 11:00 p.m. show. It wasn't *his* fault that the movie theater is a twenty-minute drive from our home and that the traffic was horrible and that even if he *had* been home by ten, which is what we'd suggested, he never could have fallen asleep that early because his body isn't programmed that way. Anyway, what was there to be done? This was *Star Wars*.

Dan was not at peak performance level when he took the SAT for the second time. Moreover, he wasn't totally off base when he claimed that he doesn't function well in the morning, regardless of what time he beds down. Recent studies confirm a fact that parents learn as soon as the first blackhead appears on the silken cheek of their firstborn: *teenagers do not function well early in the day.* The Educational Testing Service would probably have to reset all its norms if it scheduled the test for 3:00 p.m. or later. Grades might increase dramatically if high school classes were taught *after* the sun came up. Why not start the school day earlier for the younger children, who are up

48

Watsamatta U:
A Get-a-Grip
Guide to
Staying Sane
Through Your
Child's College
Application
Process

anyway? Plus, parents with jobs could actually arrive on time if older kids were home until the young ones left.

On that particular early Saturday morning, Dan managed to eke out the extra 100 points promised him. His scores were now above average, but he fell ten points shy of a jump into the league with the really good players. Just ten points and he could get attention from a higher tier of schools. Just ten points!

I'm surprised Dan didn't take up residence at a friend's house or even in a tree during the weeks he was preparing to take the exam for the third time. Either would have been preferable to living with me. I was a woman with a ten-point mission. Ten points or die!

Somehow, twisted around my brainwaves was the notion that only ten SAT points stood between my son and his Lifetime Achievement Award in running the universe. I became Simon Legree. Are you memorizing your word lists? Why aren't you memorizing your word lists? Can I help you memorize your word lists? Are you taking practice tests? Do you know you *have* to get those ten extra points? Do you know your future is at stake? *Do you know what this is costing me?*

He knew.

In my defense, I'd had confirmation that ten points could make it or break it for him. My girlfriend Ruthellen's daughter, Julie, was rejected by the University of Pennsylvania even though both her parents are alumni and her sister is a current senior. When Ruthellen called to find out why Julie was slight-ed after she had been "wooed" and led to believe by the alumni office that she was in, she was told that her daughter's SAT scores missed the mark by ten points. Ten points! Julie was denied an Ivy League education because of two vocabulary words.

"What do you think about making her take the test again?" the alumni admissions representative asked a dumbfounded Ruthellen.

"For ten points?" Ruthellen responded. "I think that feels like child abuse."

Julie is presently loving every minute of her life at the University of Michigan, where she has maintained an impressive 3.9 GPA ... the happy ending I wasn't yet ready to compute because it distracted me from focusing on those unattainable 10 points.

Dan was at peak performance level when he took the test four months later after a healthy eight hours of sleep and a quick three-hour brush-up session with his tutors. He scored 10 points below his last test scores.

I strongly encouraged him to take the test for a fourth time. How hard could it be to gain ten, now twenty lousy points? He refused—and that's the elegant way of putting it. It was over. We had to go on with our ten-point-shy lives.

Dan's friend, Joe, slept on Sunday mornings, played with the $20 CD put out by the *Princeton Review* for ten minutes a night for two weeks and scored a 1420. I am of the mind that it is possible to significantly improve your score on the SAT with practice. After all, there are a finite number of words in the English language. If you start memorizing lists of words early on, you are bound to encounter a hefty helping of those words on the test. Sustained good reading habits throughout school don't hurt either. I once caught Joe reading a Tom Clancy book on our sofa while he waited for Dan to shower. I believe that some very bright people—people who would be assets to any college or university—simply do not perform well in a standardized testing situation. It is a crime to deny these students their opportunity to thrive in a competitive academic setting. I believed this when my wallet was $2000 fatter ... and I believe it now.

50

Watsamatta U:
A Get-a-Grip
Guide to
Staying Sane
Through Your
Child's College
Application
Process

OK. The scores are in. Your child now has a number attached to him. He is the sum of his math and verbal scores and you will be surprised at how many times his number comes up. People who would never think to ask you your child's IQ or your income do not feel similarly discreet about the results of the SATs. Parents compare SAT scores as if they were stock tips.

"How did Sally do?" Billy's mother asks, petrified that Sally might have outmathed her son and thus nab the spot at Cal Tech she hoped would have Billy's name on it. Three million other students might also have outmathed Billy, but she doesn't know those students. Sally's 750 is the threat that speaks its name.

If Billy's mother learns that Sally performed disappointingly, her relief is palpable. Beating it down with potato-masher intensity in order not to look haughty, she smiles intimately and responds, "Don't worry, dear. It's just not that important. Good grades are weighted far more heavily at most schools than SAT scores." Horse manure. It's a package, ma'am!

Many parents can recite the scores of their friends' kids. I've heard conversations that last a half hour or longer on this subject. Dan couldn't tell me what many of his friends scored. I could have called their parents for that information, but what was I going to do with the knowledge of my friends' kids' SAT scores? Either I was going to eat myself up alive, which I did when I learned that Nancy's daughter, Lauren, scored a 1420 and was applying to most of the same schools that Dan had selected, or I would feel badly for another friend's kid and have to utter that ludicrous condolence line about how it doesn't matter anyway. Neither position was one I wanted to spend much time in.

There was benefit to be gained, however, by amassing SAT information from kids who had dragged themselves through the system *before* Dan. I asked every friend I have whose child was currently enrolled in college to cough up the kid's SAT scores. Later, I would race back to the *College Handbook 2001* to zero in on the college that child attended and compare the SAT score quoted to me with the SAT requirements in the directory listing. My goal, obviously, was to unearth as many examples as I could of kids who had been admitted to competitive colleges with lower SAT scores than the college declares it likes to see. Unfortunately, I found very few cases like this. Zero, actually. It appears that colleges don't lie about their SAT standards. So at least we knew the truth. The truth can set you free. As I had suspected, the Ivies would miss out on the wonder that is my handsome and talented son, 580 math, 610 verbal.

Eleven Tips for Not Letting the SAT Debilitate You

1. Even college admissions offices have their doubts about the ability of the SAT to predict academic performance in college. The California State College system may eliminate the SAT from its list of admissions criteria altogether. Your child could go to a good college on the West Coast, stay warm, and audition for *Friends* at the same time. That's where the real money is anyway.

2. Your child's SAT scores will be conversation-worthy for about forty-five minutes out of his life. Can you think of any of your adult friends whose SAT scores you know? Do you even know where your friends went to college?

3. SATs are to life as Cap'n Crunch is to
   a. nutrition
   b. naval operations
   c. Charles Laughton
   d. beer nuts

4. Could you have aced your SATs even if your parents really, really wanted you to and offered you a car to do it?

52

Watsamatta U:
A Get-a-Grip
Guide to
Staying Sane
Through Your
Child's College
Application
Process

5. Hide the movie section of the paper on the Friday night before the Saturday morning of the SATs.

6. The College Board posts one "SAT question of the day" on its Web site, www.collegeboard.com. It takes two minutes of your child's time or less to complete. If you are diligent, you can spread the SAT experience out over a period of years. For free.

7. Before you blab your child's SAT scores to the whole town, consider how you would feel if she did that with your weight.

8. Don't ask your kid's friends or your friends' kids what they scored. How will that information help you?

9. Remember: no matter how much money you spend on SAT preparation, there are people who will be spending more. If it means that much to them, let them win.

10. Leave the calculator, two No. 2 pencils, and the registration card on the floor in front of the exit to your house so your child will trip over them in the morning.

11. They tell your kids not to bring anything into the room with them during the test, but my friend Judy's son brought a small piece of his baby blanket for luck. When the proctor asked him what that frayed piece of cloth was on the desk, Scott replied, "That's Bonggie!" The proctor said, "OK, then," and walked away. Be judicious.

Addendum

As I write this addendum, the finishing touches are being lovingly applied to this book. I am one month away from seeing the tangible result of this effort, which means I am a year and a half removed from my first college adventure. Things have only gotten worse in the interim. Today I am scrambling to write my reaction to a recent *Time* magazine story, which claimed that there are children in the *third grade* who have actually taken the SAT exam at their parents' behest. Sixth and seventh graders are taking the exam in local high schools three years before they are allowed to have lockers there. Are these the same children we expect to selflessly care for us in our old age? If these kids are as bright as their parents think they are, then they know that it is not selflessness, but quite the opposite that fuels this quest for genius. Frankly, I'd be much more inclined to push the wheelchair of someone who let me spend my Saturday mornings with Alvin and the Chipmunks than I would for a parent who made me keep company with some cantankerous proctor working overtime.

In a recent *New York Times Magazine* article, sociologist William Doherty was quoted as saying, "this frenzied rush to capitalize or 'nurture' a child's potential is less parenting than it is product development." I couldn't have said it better.

Chapter 7
Any Mail for Me?

According to our bathroom scale, which sadly has never *underweighed* anything in its life, Dan has received 37¾ pounds of mail since March of his junior year. Four pounds of it came from Duke alone. Obviously, Duke has an endowment significant enough to absorb the cost of sending eight or 10 different glossy public relations brochures to students who expressed interest, but are bright enough to not follow up with an actual application.

I pored over these missives as if J.D. Salinger had come out of seclusion to write college propaganda mailings. Most of the brochures and letters didn't impart any information I hadn't already gleaned from memorizing the *College Handbook 2001,* but the pictures were gorgeous. I especially liked the way some of them seamlessly included Dan's name in the body of the brochure. One arrived camouflaged as a newspaper headlined, "Dan Whatsisname to attend Justforyou U! Campus pulls out the stops for him!" Kudos to that college! It was tacky, but he read it!

Dan received exactly no mail from Harvard or Princeton or

any of the other Ivy League schools. He was neither surprised nor disappointed.

He did receive information from many distinguished institutions of higher learning, which he summarily rejected for very sound reasons. Case Western Reserve University's name was too long. Same with Carnegie Mellon. He wanted to attend a school whose name trips lightly off your tongue or at least has a nickname that does. Oberlin could not possibly be a good school because he personally does not know anyone who goes there. I personally do, but that doesn't count. He pooh-poohed any college he had never heard of. Fortunately, this procedure eliminated many schools located in places that require long airline trips with stopovers in Houston. Unfortunately, it also eliminated some excellent schools closer to home.

I presented him with two baskets to hold the deluge, since all of the drawers in his bedroom are filled with concert ticket stubs, tennis balls, and I don't know what else because I'm afraid to fish through the old concert ticket stubs and tennis balls. One basket was to be used as the "possibility box" and one was for the discards.

"Why can't I just throw out the ones I don't want?" he wanted to know.

"I don't know," I confessed, "but keep them. You may want to look at them later."

Later never came. The discard basket is overflowing with *unopened* college mail. The brochures have oozed out onto his floor and threaten to take over the whole upstairs. Even I got sick to death of reading about majors and concentrations and faculty-student ratio and opportunities for personal discovery. They all began to sound the same. Is there anyplace where you *can't* major in psychology or play intramural sports?

Many of the large state schools do not send out information unless it's requested. Why should they? Everyone's heard

56

Watsamatta U:
A Get-a-Grip
Guide to
Staying Sane
Through Your
Child's College
Application
Process

of them and, at the price of a private education today, everyone applies to them. Dan requested information from several of these schools, which means that I e-mailed the institutions myself while he was at school. Then, when the desired packets arrived, usually *eight to ten weeks later,* he threw them unopened into the "in" basket.

"I don't have to look at these," he claimed. "I already know I'm applying."

"Then why did you order them?" I wondered.

"Your point is ...?"

Chapter 8

The Happy Family's Guide to Visiting Colleges, Part A

M y point is that you have no way of knowing what it will be about a particular college that will wrap itself around your child's psyche, but judging from my limited experience, you can be fairly sure it won't jump out from one of those classy brochures.

You have to visit. Colleges encourage you to visit. Guidance counselors encourage you to visit. They guarantee that you will notice when your child "clicks" with a certain college. He or she will simply "feel comfortable" on a particular campus without being able to express why. For those rare, highly evolved few who can not only pinpoint exactly what turns them on about a school, but also translate the "turn-on" into comprehensible language, the reasons may be surprising or disappointing. For example, faculty-student ratio, which is such a big deal in all those brochures, is rarely if ever given as the reason why a student selected the school.

When Harold, Dan, and I embarked upon our college-hunting expeditions, we were armed with expert advice, both written and verbal, on how to take our first baby steps into this

Watsamatta U:
A Get-a-Grip
Guide to
Staying Sane
Through Your
Child's College
Application
Process

new dimension in parenting. What we hadn't been adequately prepared for was the *stress*.

Having been weaned on old MGM movie musicals, I can't help it … I fantasize. I fantasized myself into a sugary revelry of what our college trips would look, feel, and taste like. I would have my darling husband and firstborn son to myself for three consecutive days. This hasn't occurred since our family consisted of only myself, my husband, and my firstborn son. I let loose an imagination that conjured breezy car trips during which we would gaily chat about our upcoming adventures and sentimentally chuckle over past escapades. I looked upon this rare opportunity to hold Dan captive, away from the demands of his social life, as a time when his understandable fears about the future or concerns about the present would surface unashamedly and wonderfully demand that I become once again the omnipotent mommy of days gone by.

I was psychologically ready for this. All we had to do was select the schools we would visit. I chose first (of course) and I selected my alma mater, Northwestern University. I wanted to show it off. I wanted Dan to fall in love with the school at which I had spent four watershed years. I wanted him to breathe the rarefied air of academia and taste from the smorgasbord of possibilities for his brilliant future. I wanted to walk with him in the rhythm that is Chicago and share a deep-dish, stuffed pizza from Giordano's. But mostly, I wanted to visit my girlfriends Sylvia and Jacki, who still live there.

On reflection, it wasn't fair to do that to him—or at least to do it to him first. Why would you test-drive a Jaguar when all you can afford is an Escort? Likewise, why would you visit the school currently rated number fourteen in the nation by *U.S. News & World Report* when your grades and scores conspire to ensure rejection? I didn't see it that way then. We were going to Northwestern and my son was Dan!

I booked the flights. I made dinner reservations at restaurants with fare that would make my two younger sons gag. I registered for a campus tour and an information session. I scheduled a "non-evaluative" interview with an admissions advisor. I made sure to book some free time into our little excursion, which would allow Dan to "get a feel" for the city he'd be living in for four years should he opt for NU. Of course, I didn't give a second thought to the minuscule possibility that *NU* might not opt for *Dan*. They'd accepted *me*, hadn't they? I've never given them the slightest cause for embarrassment or regret. What possible reason could they have for not accepting the boy whose very cells match my own? I packed good walking shoes and a skirt in case we decided to take in a show. I was pumped!

Dan asked if he could bring a friend along and I instantly plummeted back to earth with a spirit-breaking thud. Months later I realize that he desperately wants to go to college with a friend and the friend he has in mind wasn't coughing up the money for a trip to Evanston, Illinois. The friend he has in mind also has higher grades and better SAT scores than Dan. *Why would I enable this child to take the space at NU I wanted my son to occupy?* I like this kid, but *come on!*

Dan hadn't meant to wound me by acting as though our little college bonding experience wasn't as seminal to him as it was to me. Naturally my feelings were hurt anyway. I vetoed the friend proposal, pouted melodramatically and publicly for a day or two, then pulled myself together in time for us to catch the early plane.

Dan sat between Harold and me on the plane. Unless positioned behind the controls, Dan and I both fall asleep within thirty seconds of any moving vehicle's departure. Needless to say, we didn't engage in any meaningful dialogue up at 32,000 feet. He did sleep with his head on my shoulder, though, which felt a lot like bonding to me.

Watsamatta U:
A Get-a-Grip
Guide to
Staying Sane
Through Your
Child's College
Application
Process

We rented a car at the airport and drove to Evanston, which is located along the North Shore of Lake Michigan about forty minutes from Chicago. This would be an ideal time for a chat.

Chapter 9

Another College Conversation: A Reenactment

Mom

Dan? ... Dan? ... *Dan?* ... **Dan!**

Dan

Hmm?

Mom

Honey, we're going to be there in about a half hour. You have an interview in one hour. Don't you think you should wake up?

Dan

I'll get up in time.

Mom

Don't you think you should wake up *before* time?

Dan

Don't worry, Mom. I'll be awake.

Mom

I just think that when it is so important to make a good impression, you should give yourself time to pull yourself together, look alive and act interested. You aren't going to get a second chance at this. They want to see a bright, friendly, high-

62

Watsamatta U:
A Get-a-Grip
Guide to
Staying Sane
Through Your
Child's College
Application
Process

ly motivated and energetic kid, which we both know you are. Now if I were you, I would ...

Dan

Awrightawready! I'm up!

Mom

Thank you.

Dan

You're welcome. So?

Mom

So what?

Dan

So I know you woke me up because you wanted to talk to me about something. So what is it?

Mom

Nothing.

Dad

Go on. Tell him.

Mom

It's nothing. I have nothing I want to tell you.

Dad

Don't be ridiculous. You wanted to talk to him. You woke him up so you could talk to him. So talk to him.

Mom

I've changed my mind.

Dad

Oh, for crying out loud!

Dan

Geez, Mom! What is it?

Mom

If I suggest something, you're only going to yell at me, so I've decided to keep my mouth shut.

Dan

OK.

Dad

Fine.

Mom

OK, I'll tell you. I just thought it would be a good idea to maybe do a practice interview before we get there. That's all. No big deal.

Dan

You're kidding, right?

Mom

No. How could it hurt to do a run-through? I'll be the interviewer.

Dan

First of all, this isn't even a real interview. This doesn't count for anything, remember? They tell you in all their information that the interview doesn't count.

Mom

Every time someone meets you, it counts. *Every* time. Sue me. Yell at me. It counts.

Dan

And you think I'm going to sit there and pick my nose or pass wind or something? Mom, I always make a good first impression. Don't people tell you that all the time? I'm Dan.

Dad

He's Dan.

Mom

I know, sweetheart. I just want them to see the real you.

Dan

Oh, you mean not the Dan impersonator I brought along?

Mom

I knew this would happen.

Watsamatta U:
A Get-a-Grip
Guide to
Staying Sane
Through Your
Child's College
Application
Process

Dan

I'm sorry, but jeez, mom, give me some credit, won't you? I'll be fine. I don't even think they want to know about me. I think they look at this as a chance for me to ask questions about *them*.

Mom

And do you have any?

Dan

Any what?

Mom

Questions!

Dan

No.

Mom

Well, don't you think you should prepare some?

Dan

What could I possibly ask that you haven't already answered for me in great detail?

Mom

There must be something I haven't answered.

Dan

OK. How long does it take you to die if you fall into Lake Michigan in February? Is that good?

Mom

Forget about it. You're on your own, kid. Don't say I didn't offer to help.

Dan

OK, OK. I thought I'd ask about the faculty-student ratio.

Mom

Now you're talking! You'll do just fine, dear. Just be yourself.

Chapter 10

The Happy Family's Guide to Visiting Colleges, Part B.

What Interview?

B y the time we arrived on campus, Dan had morphed into his fully awake persona ... the one that is, in my judgment, irresistible. As we took a brief stroll in the vicinity of the admissions office, my heart warmed at the sight of old familiar buildings and gathering places.

Later, I would discover that, over the past twenty-three years, Northwestern has also done its share of morphing. It had always been a beautiful campus. Today it is breathtaking. Especially in the spring when tulips bloom in the Shakespeare garden and roses dot the cheeks of fresh-faced visiting high schoolers.

I couldn't wait to show Dan my old stomping grounds ... and maybe an academic building, too. But first, we had to get through the interview.

What interview? Twenty-seven years ago colleges actually wanted to *meet* the young people who professed a lifelong yearning to be a member of their academic community.

66

Watsamatta U:
A Get-a-Grip
Guide to
Staying Sane
Through Your
Child's College
Application
Process

Twenty-seven years ago they even wanted to meet kids who weren't sure where they wanted to go. Today, most large and even midsize colleges *do not grant personal interviews, period.*

At first I thought this bogus policy was just something universities submitted to the *College Handbook 2001* to discourage people who weren't yet certain that college XYZ would make it to their short list. They couldn't possibly mean that they wouldn't grant an interview to someone who demonstrated *serious* intent to apply and then to enroll if accepted.

Guess what? They mean it! My polite requests for the personal touch were denied without exception by *every* institution I contacted. Large, famous universities and many midsize, semi-famous colleges *do not grant personal interviews, period*— and those happened to be the schools we were considering.

We have thus far visited eight colleges and Dan has personally spoken with 10 admissions staff people. Seven of them were undergraduates themselves. Even if the colleges lie and consider this an interview, which they don't, how much credence would they give to the opinion of a kid two years older than the applicants? The junior interviewers could blackball your child because they disagree over which rock star is the hottest.

The catchword now is "non-evaluative." If your child is hell-bent on meeting someone personally (and most kids are because their parents tell them they are), you can request a "non-evaluative interview," which isn't an interview at all, but rather an information-gathering session. Granted, you've probably gathered this information before you made the first phone call. You had access to it by reading the campus publications. You will hear it again on your tour and a third time in the information session you will attend after your tour. If your child wants to do something new and unusual with his major, like combine marine biology with nineteenth-century English literature so he can pen his opus entitled *Moby Dickens,* he may need to meet personally with a well-informed staff member to see if this is possible. But if he wants to major in business and technology so he can move to Silicon Valley, start up a dot-com, and buy a bungalow for the price of the Chrysler Building, he would do just as well to hold his questions until the information session for the benefit of the other thousand or so kids who are also so inclined.

Despite the fact that colleges mean it when they say they *do not grant personal interviews, period*, it seems that every hopeful candidate visiting NU that day had an appointment for a "non-evaluative interview." Parents, myself included, steadfastly refuse to believe that a personal appearance means nothing ... that any admissions officer within spitting distance of our children wouldn't sprint for his or her notebook to jot down a few quick hyperboles.

So your child really *is* a number ... the sum of her GPA and her SATs and whatever point value is attached to her extracurricular activities. Colleges will boast about looking carefully at the *whole person,* but my son's whole person includes his poise, his grace under pressure, and his personal warmth. You'd think that a prerequisite for becoming a communications major—which is what Dan aspires to be—would be excellent interpersonal skills. You'd think. For all they learn from his numbers, Dan could have the panache of a canned cranberry sauce roll. All of our children's precious selves include unquantifiable, unique characteristics that make them who they are. What a shame no one has the time to notice them.

I intended this chapter to be an indictment of impersonal college admissions offices, but Mrs. Adler, Dan's guidance counselor, beseeched me to see it from the colleges' perspective. Naturally, I then decided to write this as an indictment against Mrs. Adler ... and would have if she weren't such a nice person who genuinely cares about Dan and all her students.

68

Watsamatta U:
A Get-a-Grip
Guide to
Staying Sane
Through Your
Child's College
Application
Process

The sad truth is that many competitive colleges receive up to 30,000 applications. How many people would they have to hire in order to personally interview 30,000 kids? How many hours would that take? At what cost? When I attend my husband's annual office holiday party, I make it a goal to meet four new people each year. It's the most I can handle in three hours if I want to remember them well enough to ask about their kids or their vacations at the next office function. I can't imagine having to remember more than ten or twenty kids even if it were my job to do so and even if I could take notes. How many different ways are there to write, "nice kid"? They're all nice kids. They all work hard and fight with their siblings and love nature and Jennifer Aniston. The truth hurts.

Dan was ushered into a room with four other hopefuls from four states, all of whom aspired to be engineers. I gather that engineering is a hot major. As for Dan, well, he threw a dart one day at a list Mrs. Adler handed out and his dart decided to major in communications, concentrating in the area of advertising. We think it is an excellent choice for our creative, personable son who has never scored less than 100% on an oral presentation.

Come to find out, communications is every bit as hot as engineering. It's hot because it's "way cool." Everyone's kid wants to contribute to the ghastly proliferation of media in this country, until the constant din will surely kill us all or at least cause a collective case of terminal apathy.

But back in that mahogany office, it was engineering day. It was also short kid day. Dan towered over his three interview mates.

I mentally checked off the plusses and minuses at breakneck speed before the door was closed in front of me. He's the only non-engineer in the room. That's good. It will set him apart. But it's bad if the engineers dominate the conversation and he can't wangle his way in. What is the message transmitted if a communications major can't finesse his way into a conversation with a trio of engineers? He's tall. That's good … unless he slouches self-consciously. That would be bad indeed … but unlikely. His mother is an alum. Nice plus … if he remembers to tell the non-interviewer. He may be surrounded by perfect SAT scores. Not good at all.

Harold and I took seats in the waiting room and pretended to read relevant propaganda like all the other parents. After a minute or two, a conversation erupted.

"What other schools are you visiting?" the couple from Oklahoma wanted to know.

"We have no idea," I said. "We're just beginning this process. We're here because I'm an alum and I loved it here. What about you?"

"After Northwestern we're going east to see MIT. Our oldest is a junior there on full scholarship. He's going to show William around. Then we do Princeton and Harvard. This summer we'll fly out to Cal Tech."

"William must be a very good student," I said, detesting the squat little goody-goody I had only caught the tiniest glimpse of.

"Oh, yes, he certainly is. He takes a bus to the university three days a week for four of his classes. Our local high school was no longer able to satisfy his needs."

Our local high school is no longer able to satisfy Dan's needs either, but that's because Pizza Hut terminated its contract with the cafeteria.

I didn't feel like chewing the fat anymore. Suddenly, NU's annual report of alumni giving looked fascinating to me and begged a perusal.

70

Watsamatta U:
A Get-a-Grip
Guide to
Staying Sane
Through Your
Child's College
Application
Process

Harold and I have since met many lovely, down-to-earth parents with whom we've exchanged first glances and later friendly conversation from across an admissions office waiting room. We've commiserated and shared anxieties and anecdotes. These short but pleasant associations have helped all of us take the edge off a highly stressful situation. You learn quickly how to sort the friendly, open parents from those toxic cases who stare at you until you wonder if your fly is open.

I was somewhat guarded during that first college visit. In fact, on that maiden trip I sat still as a stone, wanting to blow a hole in someone's head and not even caring if it was my own. I saw *everyone* there as competition. True, I'll probably never win any Miss Congeniality Awards, but I do consider myself personable and compassionate ... enough, anyway, to have formed many lasting and rich friendships that will carry me gently into old age. When I'm not buckling under pressure, I enjoy a good laugh. My anxiety manifested itself as aloofness on that day at NU, though, and I'd venture to guess that even Mr. Rogers would have been loath to call me his neighbor.

I wish I could go back. I wish I could tell Mr. and Mrs. William's Parents that I hope William gets into Northwestern. And into MIT also, for that matter. William was in college in high school! He *should* attend a prestigious university!

I advise parents behind me on the time line to pack lightly for college trips. And pack lightheartedness to go with those light shoes. Your child has no better chance of admittance if you sulk than if you smile. And you might meet some terrific compañeros.

Dan emerged from the room ebullient.

"Piece of cake," he boasted. "She loved me."

Lack of confidence has never made our list of things we'd like to change about Dan.

That casual debriefing was unsatisfying for me. I ached to know everything that transpired, from body language to specific questions asked. Did she write anything down or at least look like she wanted to? Did he smile? Did the engineers dominate? Did he ask about faculty-student ratio?

To my dying day, "piece of cake" will have to suffice. On to the tour.

Chapter 11
The Happy Family's Guide to Visiting Colleges, Part C

The Campus Tour

Make no mistake about it. The campus tour guide is almost completely responsible for your impression of a college. Unless the weather is rotten on the day you visit. If the weather is cold, rainy, snowy, or gray, nothing the guide can say will turn your child on to the school.

This may sound ridiculous, but ask around. Most parents will corroborate the absurd fact that most kids are unable to viscerally connect with the warm, sunny heart of a school when their feet are wet. Let's suppose, however, that you've arranged to visit a school on a sunny spring day. The good will that you and your child are likely to experience or not will most probably emanate directly from your guide. No amount of careful research, intimate conversations with admissions officers or alumni, seminars, handbooks, rankings lists, or guidance counselor advice can substitute for an hour spent with a current and usually very perky student. Plus, it's so cute how they walk backwards the whole time. Dan loved that. Occasionally they trip, but very rarely. At NYU, they walk backwards in Fifth Avenue traffic.

Campus guides tell it like it is. If you ask them about the food, they will share in no uncertain terms that it sucks, if in fact it does. They will also tell you vital information such as the size of the library collection. I always watched the faces of the high schoolers when our tour guide informed us that there were 1,000,000 or 430,000 or a mere 50,000 books in the school library. Most often the kids stared blankly into space, probably wondering if the library vending machines carry Twix bars. I attended Harvard University's graduate school. The Harvard library holdings are in the multimillions. So what? I read maybe fifty books while I was there. But I made a couple thousand trips to the vending machine.

Here's what the kids really want to know:

- Does the Dave Matthews Band or Creed ever perform here?

- Are you allowed to have a car freshman year?

- What's the punishment for getting caught drunk?

- Is the pizza in this town thick or thin crust?

- How many fraternities and sororities are on campus? How many kids join? How difficult is it to get into the good ones?

- Is there skiing within an hour's drive?

- Are the bathrooms coed?

- Can your boyfriend stay in your room overnight?

- Do you have an ultimate frisbee team?

Prospective freshmen are either too afraid of looking shallow or too deep into REM sleep to ask these questions of the admissions officers who conduct the information session that follows the tour. But face to face with a peer, these innermost, pressing concerns surface—and the way a tour guide addresses them is paramount.

74

Watsamatta U:
A Get-a-Grip
Guide to
Staying Sane
Through Your
Child's College
Application
Process

For this reason, colleges are fairly finicky about whom they select to represent them in the field. All of our tour guides were well scrubbed. Even our NYU guide seemed to have polished her nose ring for the occasion. They are always happy to answer your son's or daughter's questions, no matter how quirky, and a superior guide will sometimes share personal anecdotes, which are almost always delightful. These kids are so adorable that the rare somewhat less than adorable guides are the ones who stand out in your mind, such as a certain unnamed guide at a certain unnamed school who must have said, "You might want to keep this in mind, also" at least half a million times in the course of our hour with her. Thirty or so perfect strangers exchanged intimate winks and grins behind her back as she told us that the upholstery had just been changed in the student union and "you might want to keep this in mind, also."

We acquired factoids we were sure were edited out of the Tour Guide Manual. The administration at one college we visited would be distressed, we're sure, to learn that our guide shared the unhappy news that the previous spring some disgruntled economics majors set fire to the economics building in order to avoid taking the final exam. *I did not make this up!* This information came to us shortly after one of the deans at the same school let it slip that the college was furiously trying to figure out why they experienced a dramatic and unaccountable rise in severe depression among freshmen that year. I have a hypothesis. *They didn't like it there!*

At another school, when Dan asked if he should bring a laptop to school or if a desktop computer was the technology of choice, our guide warned him of a university-wide theft problem. Lovely.

"Laptops are the coolest," he advised. "But you have two options if you want to bring a laptop. Either you have to carry it with you *everywhere* you go, including the bathroom if you have to pee while you're in the library, or you can leave it in your dorm room and make sure that the door is locked 24-7. I personally know five kids who have had their laptops stolen."

"There is a third option," I thought to myself. "He can stay away from here." Naturally, we opted for option three.

Before my campus tours, I had assumed that a dorm room is a dorm room is a dorm room. Not true. We saw a wide variation in size and comfort of dorm rooms. Some colleges have swelled so acutely with kids that they have bought old, nearby motels and converted them to dorms with varying results. Sometimes the rooms are larger than rooms that were built with the intention of housing college students, but often they are situated quite a distance from the hub of campus life. Although a nice space to hang a hat makes any college more desirable, the accommodations rarely tip the scale one way or the other for most kids. I've seen the dorm rooms at Princeton. Trust me on this.

At Northwestern that day, *everything* tipped the scale in favor of the school, except perhaps the reputation of the winter weather. OK, I'm an alum. It's natural and easy to accuse me of a bias in favor of my alma mater. I suspect, however, that anyone who puts Northwestern on his college visitation itinerary will agree that my opinion of the sheer beauty of the place is not exaggerated.

First of all, NU is situated on a lake that is the size of an ocean. When I attended twenty-seven years ago, we could sit on the beach to study for our spring exams. I don't know if there is much beach left anymore, because of all the buildings that have sprung up on landfills since the early '70s, but at least there is a breathtaking *view* of the beach. On the May morning that we arrived, students were rollerblading down paved paths built expressly for that purpose. They were picnicking under 200-year-old trees and sharing burgers at outdoor café tables.

76

Watsamatta U:
A Get-a-Grip
Guide to
Staying Sane
Through Your
Child's College
Application
Process

The new, state-of-the-art athletic center left Dan frothing at the mouth. If Mozart ever rises from the dead, he'll choose to conduct at NU's grand, new, acoustically perfect performing arts center. There is even an art gallery *on campus*. In my mother's words, "Pish posh." What is there to say? The place is gorgeous. Schools with tuitions that cost as much as Belgium usually are.

And Northwestern is in Evanston, Illinois, a charming, small city that used to be dry but is no longer. *And* it is forty minutes from Chicago, which was Frank Sinatra's and everyone else's "kind of town," ... home to Second City, the Cubs, and I'm sure a stop on the Dave Matthews Band tour. Our bright, perky, definitely-on-the-right-side-of-adorable guide, whose face glowed with the contentment of a very blessed child, walked us through acres of academia, as all along the way you could hear the hearts of the tour mates beating, "Take me. Take me. Take me."

Guidegirl answered all questions put to her with honesty and humor. Her excitement about her college experience spilled onto all of us, making even the oldest among us wish for a second chance to go to school and appreciate it for the grand opportunity it is, instead of accepting it cavalierly as we did the first time around, when many of us just thought it was owed to us because we were alive.

Here's a valuable tip. When you visit colleges, if you're inclined to take a look at Northwestern or one of the other similarly beautiful and well-endowed schools, and I know there are many, *don't do it first!* The lyric, "How ya gonna keep 'em down on the farm after they've seen Paree?" can easily be adapted to "How ya gonna make 'em happy with small-college-in-industrial-town after he's seen NU?"

OK, maybe I *am* slightly biased. No matter, Dan was a goner. *N-U* is how he spelled college. Unfortunately, the admissions officer at the information session that followed our tour spelled it s-t-r-a-i-g-h-t A-s o-r c-l-o-s-e t-o i-t.

Chapter 12
Any Questions?

The information session is a one- to one-and-a-half-hour dog and pony show that colleges present instead of meeting with you personally. By the time you've read the college booklets and brochures and course catalogs, had a non-evaluative interview for the purpose of gathering information, and taken a campus tour, the information session is unbearably redundant, although some of the videos are nice and once in a while you see a kid of someone you know on camera.

The visiting seniors at the information session sit much as they do at that first college seminar night ... comatose. They're tired. They've toured for an hour, they've turned on the personality for the non-interviewer, and they've had all of their pressing food, drink, car, and concert questions answered. Now they whine about wanting to go back to the hotel for a swim or a nap.

Their parents, meanwhile, sit poised to glean even the smallest bit of information they might have missed during the past six months of information-gathering activities. They are in search of the bit to put this college over the top. Some sit with pencils raised or Palm Pilots at the ready.

78

Watsamatta U:
A Get-a-Grip
Guide to
Staying Sane
Through Your
Child's College
Application
Process

They're all uniformly humiliated by their kids' apparent lack of interest. On average, I witnessed four yawns per information session we attended. Embarrassingly, one was emitted by my own kid. I didn't give a thought to the possibility that the presenter might find my dramatic reaction to Dan's yawn even ruder than the yawn itself. Yawning, after all, is an involuntary act. On the other hand, if you really try hard you can control the urge to swear and point your finger to within a millimeter of your child's nose.

I wasn't the only mother hissing, pinching, or elbowing her child into consciousness that afternoon, but that sad fact doesn't justify the behavior. I'm the one who should have been pinched.

The presenters themselves are not fazed. After conducting this session four times a week, twice or three times a day, they are able do it on automatic pilot. Presenters are always enthusiastic and always, *always* young. Thirty, it seems, is over the hill in the college admissions information session presenter job profile. The burnout must come on as quickly as that economics building took fire when torched.

Usually, the presenter makes every student in the room recite his or her name, city of origin, high school, and intended major. This is the last time the students will speak before dozing off. Several parents contort their heads and necks. These would be the parents of communications, engineering, or business majors who are trying to sneak a peek at the sea of competition. The parents of the sole English or foreign language major stare straight ahead or tie their shoes.

The meat of the session is then presented.

Fifteen Things You Should Know About College Information Sessions

1. Your child should try to get good grades in high school. Duh. Aren't you glad to be hearing, at the end of her junior year in

high school, that the best way to increase her chances of being admitted to the college of her choice is to get very high grades in a very challenging program? Most competitive schools want to see a 3.4 GPA or higher. Northwestern is in the "or higher" category.

2. SAT scores aren't weighed as heavily as grades, but they do count, and a minimum of 1200 would be very nice. Northwestern wants more than "very nice"—and gets it.

3. *All* colleges look for well-rounded students. Join a club or play a sport. If possible, be the best in the country at it.

4. Giving back to your community demonstrates good moral fiber. Take a day off from being the best at your sport or talent in order to give blood or sing at a nursing home.

5. *All* colleges have an excellent faculty-student ratio.

6. *All* faculty at *all* colleges are accessible to the students. Some even go out for coffee with undergrads. I have a hard time picturing Saul Bellow or Al Gore shooting the breeze over latte with my kid at Starbucks. *All* faculty have regular office hours.

7. *All* faculty members at *all* colleges are recognized experts in their individual fields of endeavor. Most not only enjoy teaching undergraduates but are *required* to do so.

8. *All* colleges boast of hundreds of opportunities for study abroad in hundreds of fascinating countries, to which most parents have never traveled.

9. *All* colleges can provide you with a plethora of stimulating internship experiences, both paid and unpaid.

10. At *all* colleges, the placement office has an excellent record of placing students in exciting and glamorous jobs after graduation.

11. Most graduates at the college of your choice opt for more education at the graduate level. Most are successful in gaining admittance to the graduate school of their choice.

80

Watsamatta U:
A Get-a-Grip
Guide to
Staying Sane
Through Your
Child's College
Application
Process

12. *All* colleges have famous alumni, although some won't divulge who they are. The not-quite-famous ones are scattered around the globe and provide invaluable networking opportunities.

13. Colleges are need-blind when handing out acceptances. None give preferential treatment in the admissions process to parents who can foot the whole, absurdly ridiculous bill.

14. There are more than 250 clubs and student-run organizations on campus that receive some financial support from the Activities and Organizations Board. If you don't find a club that caters to your fly-fishing needs, simply get four other fly-fishers together and a new club will be formed and partially funded.

15. Colleges love to brag about small class size. Small classes are a very important selling point for parents, if not for their children. Dave Barry wrote in a column last year that Harvard is such a top-of-the-line school they have *zero* kids in a class!

The hand Dan usually raises remained rooted to his right knee during our information session at Northwestern, as did the hands of most of the other hopefuls. He had been charming and talkative during his non-evaluative interview and the tour, but now he was all charmed and questioned out. Getting yelled at hadn't helped either.

The presenter closed the information session by telling us that they received more than 30,000 applications last year for 3,000 spots. They fully expect that number to increase this year. A collective sigh was emitted and we were ushered out, all of us now looking ever so slightly green with nausea. The least they could have done was offer us a cookie and some juice.

The comments in the lobby are uniform. As they leave, most parents compute the odds. If every school receives 30,000 or more applications, to how many schools must your son or daughter apply in order to be certain of admission to one? With those numbers is there even such a thing as a safety school any more?

So where does all this leave you and your child? Intellectually, you realize that your kid will thrive at any one of hundreds of colleges. In your gut, though, you wonder if he or she will be accepted *anywhere*.

The information you glean from the information session is all curiously positive. No college will tell you that it has a severe drug problem, or that its courses are Mickey Mouse, or that no one who ever graduated from there admits to it.

Despite all the facts and figures at his disposal, your child is likely to make a decision based solely on gut instinct. He liked the sound of a conversation he overheard in the cafeteria, or she didn't like the fact that the nearest restaurant was five miles away and Thai, or he doesn't know at all why he liked it—he *just does!* Try to let this be OK. After all, all of our crazy children are around due to our own gut instincts; there's no *rational* reason to put yourself through parenthood. If you've come this far, your instincts were good. Trust that theirs will be likewise. (And if I had been able to do that, I'd be writing short stories for *The New Yorker* right now instead of this book.)

Despite the stillness, the yawns, and the anxiety on parade, the positive energy about Northwestern in that room on that day was palpable and experienced by all. It was disheartening indeed to realize, as most all of us did, that only a few lucky ones among our children would be invited to watch the leaves turn golden in the Evanston autumn.

Chapter 13

The Happy Family's Guide to Visiting Colleges, Part D

The Aftermath

We didn't look like a particularly happy family that evening at dinner. Over huge slabs of Midwestern beef, we shared our individual reactions to the day, which felt like it had begun a month before. Northwestern had everything Dan was looking for in a school—except a lenient admissions policy. My B student had about as much chance of being admitted to Northwestern, even with my alumna status, as I have of winning the Preakness on Mister Ed. *When did this happen to Northwestern?* It had always been an excellent institution of higher learning, but it had always been within reach of your garden-variety, above-average, highly talented person. Today, above average is Jello. NU wants crème brûlée.

Valuable tip: parents who want their child to aspire to a top-drawer college should visit the campus well *before* spring of the junior year. What point is there to falling in love with a school when you have no time to bring your statistics up to the level that the school demands? How much more inspiring it would be to shepherd your newly minted high school freshman to

Xanadu while he's still got a clean slate and say, "This is where you can go if you work your ass off for the next four years," than it is to castigate that child a few years after the fact, "If only you had listened to me, this could have been yours." College is an amorphous concept for your average fourteen-year-old, like death or home equity loans. Let him or her smell the rarefied air of a top-drawer school in order to make it a reality worth striving for.

As the months ticked by, I would learn that, like Northwestern, most colleges are more competitive now than they ever were. Most receive more applications than ever before from more academically talented kids than ever before. You could just kill yourself. But I wasn't quite tuned into this fact that night at Morton's Steakhouse. That night I had to direct my energy solely toward letting go of NU.

We sat at the table trying to take the day in stride. "I suppose," Harold mused, "he could get in if we endowed a chair." If only we'd thought of that before we'd decided to go for a third child and a house.

Dan and I have very different ways of coping with feelings of helplessness or disappointment. Like his father, Dan chooses to swallow them whole and move on. I have to masticate on mine for awhile … chew them until they are reduced to a pulp and then suck on them and let them slowly ooze down, down, into my innards. This clash of modi operandi is hardly conducive to enjoying a 5,000-calorie meal.

I could simply not stop myself from saying pointless things like "Did you ever see such a gorgeous basketball court?" or "How about that program they have where, if you get really good grades in undergraduate school, you could possibly move right into their business school in your senior year? Isn't that coooool?"

How exactly did I expect Dan to respond to this? "Yes,

84

Watsamatta U:
A Get-a-Grip
Guide to
Staying Sane
Through Your
Child's College
Application
Process

Mom. Please pass me the steak knife. I want to slit my throat now so I won't ever be a disappointment to you again." Would that have made me happy?

Harold attempted to change the subject numerous times, but I was stuck in the quicksand of dashed hopes and I was sinking fast.

I knew, even as I fretted, that if I couldn't summon up a genuine positive attitude, I had no business accompanying them on any further college junkets. Dan will attest to the fact that on our subsequent excursions I developed the positive attitude from hell. I am Little Mary Sunshine now. But that night I was Sylvia Plath. The world had faded to black.

In Chicago, when the world turns dark, you go to Second City, which we did after dinner and had a delightful time. Dan let loose and laughed raucously nonstop. I noticed in the program that three of the comedians were NU graduates, but I managed, due to great reserves of personal fortitude, to not point this out to him. They force you to be quiet in the theater anyway, unless you're laughing. Laughter is acceptable. And of course, the best medicine. I think college admissions offices should get some drama majors to put on little improvisational comedy shows for visitors. It would certainly help to lighten things up.

Something else positive came from our trip to Chicago, other than the fact that I got to visit with my good old buddies, Sylvia and Jacki, both of whom were instantly smitten with my fair son. Unfortunately, their opinions of him matter as much to NU as mine do. Dan had brought along some Spanish homework he'd been struggling with, planning to complete it on the plane between naps. He'd been assigned to read a Spanish short story and write a synopsis. Now, at midnight in Chicago, time was running out. He would have to force himself awake in order to grapple with this very challenging piece of foreign literature. We decided to work in the lounge because the bed in the room would be too great a temptation to resist after the two days we'd packed into one. As we wended our way to our table, we couldn't help overhearing the bartender engaged in heated discussion with a customer. *In Spanish!* It was midnight on a Tuesday. The lounge was empty, except for the two Latinos. Did the bartender have anything better to do? Did the customer? Dan got an A. Too late for Northwestern, but an A nonetheless.

Ten Tips for Visiting Colleges, as if You Really Need Them

1. Your college visitation is a business trip. You are destined for disappointment if you treat it like a family vacation or an intimate bonding experience. Better to be surprised if it becomes either of those things.

2. Even if your child doesn't act nervous, he or she probably is. College is a *huge* step toward independence. Be sensitive to this by not calling him your baby in front of people.

3. Bring good reading material.

4. Your child is likely to make his decision about a school in twenty seconds or less and then she will be done. Done is done. Lucky is the parent who can convince a child to "give it a chance" after her mind is made up. The rest of us can only hope the hotel gets HBO.

5. If you haven't already paid for airline tickets, reschedule your trip if you wake up and it's raining.

6. Your child is only capable of being who he is. If that's not good enough for you, ask if you can borrow your local honor student and take him.

7. Your time is better spent visiting the athletic center than the library.

Watsamatta U:
A Get-a-Grip
Guide to
Staying Sane
Through Your
Child's College
Application
Process

8. The ethernet is a good thing.

9. Slouching, yawning, scratching, snoozing, and daydreaming don't seem to have an impact on the admissions officer giving the lecture. Half of them are talking in their sleep anyway.

10. The refreshments at some universities are better than at others.

Chapter 14
So What's Plan B?

After our Northwestern experience, Harold and I decided to do as the books advise and take the lead from Dan about which schools to visit. Unfortunately, even though he'd resigned himself to the fact that neither Duke nor Northwestern would ever appear on his résumé, his "backups" still seemed a mite grandiose.

The University of Virginia, or UVA as he affectionately called it, as though it was already home to him, topped his list of "schools to try since I'm not trying Duke." We were incredulous. Apparently, the child-rearing gurus we had pooh-poohed so many years ago are occasionally right on target. If you tell your child often enough that he is perfection on earth, there's a fairly good chance that he actually will develop a healthy sense of self-esteem. So what do we do now? Tell him we lied, we really don't think he's all that terrific after all? Not on your life, because we still believe he *is* all that terrific. But how much time, money, and energy do we invest in chasing pipe dreams?

After much head scratching, I decided to try the straightforward approach by simply calling the admissions offices at

88

Watsamatta U:
A Get-a-Grip
Guide to
Staying Sane
Through Your
Child's College
Application
Process

UVA, telling them all about Dan, and asking for an honest answer as to whether or not we'd be wasting our time to visit, since we have neither family nor friends in Virginia and therefore can't kill two birds with one stone by scheduling a visit. Someone told me once that a guidance counselor had told her that it's perfectly acceptable to call admissions offices to ask such questions. Understandably, the receptionists are not allowed to give you a definite yes or no to the "Will my child get in?" question, but if you're lucky enough to get a human and not a menu on the other end of the line, sometimes you can kiss up and elicit a less than totally evasive answer. This seemed like a perfectly logical idea to me, especially since I had no intention of divulging my real name.

I placed the call and a real human being answered ... I mean a *real* human being with feelings and a sense of humor and everything. I explained that my son would very much like to attend the University of Virginia, but that we'd like to get an idea of his chances for acceptance before dashing down there like little ants hoping to move rubber tree plants. I recited Dan's GPA, SAT scores, and extracurriculars in a monotone, hoping to sound neither boastful nor apologetic. She responded with the loveliest hint of a Southern drawl.

"By any chance has your son spent any time in Bolivia vaccinating underprivileged children in the past year?" she asked without so much as a chuckle.

"No, but he played bingo with the residents of Shadybrook Nursing Home on Christmas Day."

"Given his numbers, it would have to be Bolivia or someplace like that in order for his application to be placed in the positive pile."

You have to like a woman like that. I reported back to Dan verbatim and we eighty-sixed UVA.

We were eliminating schools from our list at breakneck speed. Trouble is, we weren't replacing them with any real possibilities.

There are people you can hire, called "professional college counselors," who can help you form your list. They can cost up to $30,000 in affluent areas of the country, such as New York City. That's two years' tuition at Penn State! We chose not to employ a professional college counselor, even though I hire someone to do almost everything else, such as cleaning out the septic tank and painting the shutters and my fingernails. Next time I'll seriously consider obtaining professional counsel— even if we have to rent out the house and live in the garage to do it. There is simply too much information to weed through by yourself and too much inherent angst in the process. Also, the perfect college for your child might be one you've never heard of or you've heard of and forgotten about. (Mrs. Adler, as I've said, is warm and friendly and eager to help. And she does as much as her schedule allows her to, given her roster of 400 seniors to place.)

Harold and I offered numerous suggestions to Dan, all of which he summarily rejected for reasons we couldn't fathom, such as "because."

Finally, one starry night in June, we dragged Dan from his safe haven on the basement sofa and sat him down at the kitchen table for an emergency summit with the goal of systematically selecting eight schools for visitation. We refused to let him retire for the night before compiling a list that included two safety schools, four probables, and two reach schools. Imagine his delight at the opportunity to spend quality time with his parents in this way!

We plodded our way through his criteria.

1. The school had to be located in or near a reasonably sized city stocked with good restaurants, concerts, sporting events,

90

Watsamatta U:
A Get-a-Grip
Guide to
Staying Sane
Through Your
Child's College
Application
Process

and other opportunities to deplete one's parents' last reserves of cash.

2. The school had to have decent sports teams.

3. California was out. That was our dictum. Kids who leave the East Coast to attend school in California never come back.

4. The Midwest was out, with the exception of Chicago. Too cold. Too flat. Too complicated to get home. No surfing opportunities.

5. The school must have an excellent communications program.

6. Name recognition is nice. (As we evolved, this mattered less.)

7. He had to spot a minimum of three pretty girls on campus during a visit.

By 1:00 in the morning, Northwestern was past history, along with our family trip to the Grand Canyon and our twin goldfish, Fred and Ted. We had formulated a list of eight schools, which I will not be sharing. There were two private schools we all thought he'd have a good shot at and six large, public institutions, two that we considered to be reaches, two reasonable matches, and two that were as sure as anything can be in this crazy college-hunting climate.

Dan and Harold skipped up to bed, but I sat immobile at the kitchen table, drained and experiencing a nagging discomfort in the pit of my stomach. The schools we had selected were all "hot schools." Whenever you ask a friend where his or her child is applying to school, be that child the valedictorian or plain ol' Phil, you can bet that at least one of these eight names will be mentioned.

The Boston schools are the hottest of the hot. Practically every school in Boston makes the hot list. For years Boston has been "the place" to be a student. We were told on one of our Boston tours that one out of every five people in that city is a student. I believe that's because only eighteen- to twenty-two-year-old kids are willing to live in squalor or mooch off their parents. Those who actually have to support themselves or a family move out to the surrounding areas. I thought New York City was expensive until I tried to find a reasonably priced hotel room in Beantown. The cost of living is astronomical in Boston, which explains why even seniors often live on campus and why the private schools get away with charging upwards of $30,000 a year for an education that may lead to a Nobel Prize down the road but more likely will not.

I determinedly headed upstairs and shook both Dan and Harold awake in order to make a case for putting one more school on the list, an obscure one in desperate need of students, perhaps in the hills of North Dakota somewhere. Request denied. Time will tell.

Chapter 15
So Your Kid Wants to Play Sports in College

Harold and I have learned all we know about sports from our two oldest sons. Prior to their births, the last athletic feat anyone in either of our families had executed was a forty-year walk through the desert to the Holy Land more than 5,000 years ago. I'm pretty sure I had never been to a live baseball game before the 1988 Little League season opener. Today I could write a book or two about my experiences as a soccer mom, a baseball mom, and a basketball mom, but Dan is a tennis player, so for purposes of continuity I will limit myself to the ups and downs of the tennis racket (and I don't mean the thing you hit the ball with).

Like going to college in Boston and declaring a major in communications, playing tennis is a very "hot" thing to do, which Dan didn't realize at the age of two when he pulled an old racquetball racket from the bowels of the garage and began to hit balls against Harold's new Toyota. He'd certainly never seen either one of us hit a ball with a racket or heard us discussing the outcome of Wimbledon or seen me shop for one of those cute little outfits with the bloomers. He discovered tennis all by himself.

When Dan was five, his grandfather assessed his eye/hand coordination and, without any personal experience, determined that tennis lessons were in order because my son had a natural gift for hitting fuzzy yellow balls over nets. I took Dan for his first lesson when he was five and a half and immediately noticed that I was several years behind the eightball in getting started. There were two- and three-year-olds on the courts, hitting balls in between wetting their diapers! So what? I had every confidence that my son would catch up to these kids on the court—just as I knew that these kids would, within the year, catch up to Dan on the toilet.

In the beginning I would bring a book to read while he was taking his lesson. Once or twice I even had the audacity to leave the club and do some solo shopping. When you are a stay-at-home mom of a child who gave up naps at ten months old, a free hour late in the afternoon once a week is a gift from God. Too tired at night to read so much as the nutrition label on my energy bar, I relished a weekly midday opportunity to keep my vocabulary in fair working order.

This noble, but obviously misguided attempt at maintaining some semblance of selfhood rendered me a pariah at the racket club. The other mothers, fluent in lobs and crosscourts and overheads, glued their noses to the observation window so they could coach their kids telepathically. It became clear to my athletically challenged psyche early on that these kids were not playing tennis merely as a recreational sport so they'd have something enjoyable to do upon retirement sixty-some years later. Rather, they were being groomed. They were gaining the edge they would need to play competitively in tournaments or college or on the pro circuit. What an awakening it was!

I had been a child actress back home in upstate New York, strutting my stuff in all the high school and community productions and giving my parents much *naches* (refer to page one for definition). I lived for drama. I taught drama and directed plays

94

Watsamatta U:
A Get-a-Grip
Guide to
Staying Sane
Through Your
Child's College
Application
Process

for fifteen years before giving it all up for a glamorous dual career as a starving writer and personal slave. I have known my share of stage parents, parents who count their children's lines in the play and scream at you if they don't add up to the lines of their child's best friend. I've had mothers bribe me for a solo for little Susie, dash onstage during rehearsal to tie a hair ribbon or inject a piece of advice, mothers who ... well, you get the grisly picture.

No stage parents I have ever known or have ever ejected from rehearsal have held a candle to the overbearing sports parents I met at tournaments.

Has any parent of an athlete *not* seen an altercation occur on the tennis court or baseball diamond or soccer field between a parent and a coach? Has anyone *not* seen a Little League coach go berserk at an umpire for a questionable call or at his own kid for vegging out in left field? Parental behavior has become so deplorable that some communities have begun taking preemptive measures. The town of Jupiter, Florida, for example, now requires all parents to attend a community-sponsored class in sportsmanship *before* they are allowed to register their tykes for the township leagues.

I have very strong opinions about what has become of children's athletics and all athletics in this country. I thought the whole purpose was to keep our bodies strong and healthy and to learn good sportsmanship. Silly me!

Back to tennis. Those mothers were not off base (unlike sports, sports *metaphors* come easily to me) by compulsively watching and then dissecting their young children's lessons. Watching and dissecting is what it takes to make a star and, if you're serious about grooming an athlete who will compete past puberty, it would be beneficial to teach him or her how to accept criticism and develop a killer instinct early in the game—the tennis game and the tennis *game*. Our lack of tennis savvy (so vast that we didn't know how to keep score until Dan had been playing for three years) was a distinct disadvantage throughout his formative playing years. Without knowledge, skill, or courts, it's impossible to give your child the supplemental coaching he or she needs outside of weekly lessons. Unless you pay for it, of course. Ignorance doesn't work against you if your pockets are really deep.

It's easy to spend the equivalent of one year's college tuition *each year* on trying to keep your child on a level playing field with his competitors. Deepak had his own full-time private coach nestled comfortably on his Dad's payroll. This is less extraordinary than you might think. Harold and I have sat motionless through many tournaments trying to overhear tips from Dan's opponents' coaches. Private coaching alone can cost $20,000 annually.

If your child is serious about college tennis, playing on the high school team won't cut the mustard. He or she must hold a USTA ranking, preferably in the low digits, like number one. The USTA sponsors junior tournaments on a district, sectional, regional, and national level. Your child must work his or her way up through the system. The top USTA national players either go pro or choose to play for the top college tennis teams, such as Stanford University, which happens to have a somewhat respectable academic reputation as well.

District tournaments take a big bite out of your weekend, but at least you know where the local deli is so you can get lunch. And every so often, you can get home between matches to check on your laundry. Once your child advances to the sectional and regional levels, travel becomes necessary. Should they choose to do so, dedicated families can be on the road almost every weekend of the year, dragging dependent younger siblings along begrudgingly, or leaving them home with babysitters, or splitting up the family into tennis and non-tennis components. On weekends when mom and dad are committed elsewhere, private drivers can be hired at a respectable hourly wage to accompany minors. How Trump-

96

Watsamatta U:
A Get-a-Grip
Guide to
Staying Sane
Through Your
Child's College
Application
Process

like to arrive at a tournament with your private coach *and* your personal chauffeur!

I don't believe there is another sport that demands so much travel. Of course my day doesn't usually include fraternizing with high school football players, so I haven't asked anyone directly, but I suspect that few of them spend much time playing football several hundred miles from home. One of my friends has a son who is a starting running back in college. Aside from his regular high school away games, the farthest he ever traveled for football was to the pantry for nacho chips during the Monday night game. I don't even know if there is such a thing as a private football coach.

Of course, there's always the possibility that your child will lose in the first round of the tournament after you've driven for eight or nine hours. In that case, you have the choice of paying for a hotel for the night, which will be a miserable experience because everyone is so depressed, or you can drive back home for eight or nine hours, which won't be a walk in the park either.

Real tennis parents ... parents who can tell whether a ball is in or out of bounds from three blocks away, sit at the tournaments with fancy forms on clipboards. I've never seen one of these forms close up, but I gather they are used to record every point, because after the matches, I've often witnessed family caucuses where testy parents give an exhausted adolescent a play-by-play.

"The third point in the fourth game of the second set should have been a crosscourt groundstroke. What the hell did you think you were doing by lobbing it?"

"I don't know, Dad. Trying to win, I guess."

I heard one father, after a particularly discouraging loss, inform his son that upon arriving home he was to proceed directly to the tennis courts and remain there until he hit one thousand balls. Dad was dead serious. One thousand balls for losing the match. Dan got an ice cream sundae for losing his.

Weekly hotels, restaurant meals, tournament fees, ball machines, a thousand balls ... it's not a sport for the faint of pocketbook. And I haven't even mentioned backyard tennis courts. Did you ever know a high school football player to have his own field at home? Dan, on the other hand, knows several kids whose parents decorated the back forty with private courts even before the dot-coms made that sort of thing possible.

Even if you have a view of your personal court from your bedroom, you can't use it when it's collecting snow. Kids who live in Florida or Southern California have more than a tan separating them from their northern counterparts. The best tennis schools and camps are in the South and booked year-round. We sent Dan to a Florida camp for a week over spring break once. There, he met kids who had spent the winter months playing outdoors by day and studying with private tutors into the starlit evenings. Yes indeedy, he'll play in college. No doubt in *my mind*.

I suppose we could call Dan's tennis instructor a private coach if we were so inclined. We do, after all, pay him by the hour for private lessons and he does, after all, care a lot about Dan. Sadly for him, the most we could handle during Dan's crucial formative years was two hours per week. That alone comes to $400 a month.

We were willing to support Dan's tennis career enthusiastically and financially, but not to the extent that it would either cause us to neglect our other children or force us to eliminate family vacations or other such memory-making activities. We traveled some, but never to places that necessitated a plane ride and not frequently enough to gain entry into the inner circle of tennis families. Dan played hard when he played, but he never hit a thousand balls in a day and he rarely passed up an oppor-

98

Watsamatta U:
A Get-a-Grip
Guide to
Staying Sane
Through Your
Child's College
Application
Process

tunity to hang out with his friends in order to practice his serve.

Sports are taken so seriously that when Dan played for his private school varsity team in his freshman year while he was still in braces, I was told that it was acceptable to miss an academic subject in order to go to the orthodontist, but that missing tennis practice after school would result in extremely negative consequences. I'm sorry, *I don't understand.* I don't speak that language. Miss the biology test but not the scrimmage?

Consequently, we all got out of tennis what we put into it. Dan was a tough competitor. He has enough trophies to make dusting his dresser a pain in the rear. He played second singles for his high school varsity team for four years, but he has no national ranking. He hasn't even played many sectional tournaments. How could he? He runs food at a local bar and grill on Saturday nights and needs the money for CDs.

Still, with our naiveté firmly in place, we set out to learn about qualifying for a college tennis team.

It's very easy to screw up this process. One misplaced phone call at the inappropriate time earns you some kind of punishment from the National Collegiate Athletic Association (NCAA), although I can't remember what kind or how severe.

Most of What You Need to Know About Playing Sports in College

1. You must register for the NCAA clearinghouse. There are major consequences for failing to do this, but no rewards if you do it and on time. It behooves you to meet the deadline or something very bad will happen. The deadline is fall of the senior year.

2. Learn the gross and fine distinctions among Division I, II, and III schools. There are many factors that separate the schools, such as scholarship money, size, and I don't remem-

ber what else. I just remember that whatever I thought was a
Division I school wasn't, for a reason that never made sense to
me. I also remember there's almost no money available for
men's tennis unless you play like Pete Sampras or Andre
Agassi, both of whom never went to college so they could
spend all of their time playing.

3. Sports etiquette differs depending on which division you
are hoping to gain entry to. You must not violate the calendar
or those bad things they never elucidate will happen to you.
No contact with a college coach is permitted at all prior to July
1 after your child's junior year in high school. Once the communication ban is lifted, there are about a trillion rules and
regulations about calling, visiting, what brochures a coach can
give you or not give you, what constitutes a contact, what topics of conversation are not permitted, how many phone calls
you can make in a month .... I think the Green Berets have
fewer rules and regulations.

The NCAA handbook is so anal you can read it just for
your own amusement. For example, "contact" is defined as
"any face-to-face meeting between a college coach and you or
your parents, during which any of you say more than 'hello.'
Also, any face-to-face meeting that is prearranged or that
occurs at your high school or competition or practice site is a
contact, regardless of the conversation. These contacts are not
permissible 'bumps.'" The writing isn't *The Merchant of Venice,*
but for some reason it strikes me as cute.

Here's another favorite excerpt. "In Division 1 football, an
institution's coaches may telephone you once during the
month of May of your junior year in high school and then not
again until September 1 of your senior year in high school.
Also, an institution's football coaches can telephone you as
often as they wish during the period forty-eight hours before
and forty-eight hours after 7 a.m. on the initial signing date for
the National Letter of Intent. Outside of a contact period, a

100

Watsamatta U:
A Get-a-Grip
Guide to
Staying Sane
Through Your
Child's College
Application
Process

football coach may only telephone you once a week." It's easier to arrange a lunch date with Madonna.

NCAA has evaluation periods, quiet periods, and dead periods. Keep track of them. There are yellow copies, blue copies, and white copies of everything. Keep track of them, too.

I am not an anal person. I am an oral person. This NCAA handbook sent me speeding to Starbucks for a giant maple scone and a café mocha. Anyone who can jump through the hoops I describe and still function in other areas of life such as eating or sleeping deserves to be a college athlete or the parent of one. Natural selection wins out every time.

By July 1 after his junior year, Dan was still considered an "unrecruited prospective student-athlete." He would be responsible for initiating contact with the athletic departments of the colleges to which he would be applying. Dan mailed out ten letters of inquiry requesting information about the men's tennis program. In our experience, only the coaches who are genuinely interested in your child actually respond to this inquiry. "Genuinely interested" means they've heard of your son or daughter through the sports grapevine. We received a few letters that said in essence, "Don't bother contacting us unless you are ranked in the top ten regionally. Thank you for your interest and goodbye." It is unpleasant and downright rude to respond to a kid this way, but it does your child a big favor right from the get-go. It never hurts to know when you're barking up the wrong tree.

One of those ten letters resulted in an invitation to spend some time visiting with the tennis coach. We were thrilled. Dan had been invited to visit the coach at his first choice school. This was an opportunity for Harold and me, whose sole athletic accomplishments in college were marching to protest the Vietnam War and swaying to the Grateful Dead, to see in living color what life as a college athlete is all about.

Harold, Dan, and I spent a pleasant weekend at a large, private university in New England, which included a crisp autumn afternoon with the tennis coach. Should Dan actually attend that college and actually make the team, he would be spending only about eight more weekends there in a year than we did on that visit. In addition to loving tennis, it's essential for the college student-athlete to love sitting on a bus, because there he or she will sit for as many as twenty-six collegiate weekends, traveling back and forth between competitions. Most colleges are in session for only thirty-four or thirty-five weekends a year!

The rookie college tennis star would be well advised to develop instant and profound feelings of warm friendship for his teammates. They are sure to be his primary social connections for four years. My guess is that only war necessitates this kind of male bonding. Unlike other college sports, which take place either in the fall, in the winter, or in the spring, the men's tennis season stretches through the academic year. We began to have minor doubts about this college tennis thing.

The daily schedule is as grueling as the weekend tournament load. Practice takes place every day from 1:00 to 4:00 and you must be there. If some celebrated professor, whose class your child is dying to take, offers it only at 2:00 p.m., your son or daughter will be scouring the course registration guide for a substitute course and may end up with Persian rug embroidery, if that's the only course that allows him his practice time. If his girlfriend (should he manage to meet and hold onto one) suggests a romantic, Love Story-ish romp through the snow in the quad on a blustery winter afternoon, he can expect to disappoint her. We began to have serious doubts about this college tennis thing. This tennis thing would require almost as many hours as motherhood.

Of course on the positive side, college student-athletes are treated like kings. I remember accidentally stumbling into the

102

Watsamatta U:
A Get-a-Grip
Guide to
Staying Sane
Through Your
Child's College
Application
Process

football cafeteria once while I was at Northwestern. Those behemoths were ingesting steaks the size of groundhogs, with small, two-liter sides of mashed potatoes. Down the hall, the rest of us were picking unrecognizable vegetables out of our ground beef surprise. Northwestern's football team at that time was a laughingstock. They hadn't been to the Rose Bowl since 1949 and were teased about being number eleven in the Big Ten. Their sorry stats could not be attributed to malnutrition.

Athletes at the school we visited and, we deduced, at most schools are provided with private tutoring should they fall behind in their studies due to their sports commitments. They are given a private room for study in the athletic facility. And they get those nifty jackets with the school letters on them. The leads in the plays aren't granted recognition of this kind. My reward for appearing in a musical sophomore year while keeping my grades up was mononucleosis.

All the way home we weighed the costs and rewards of playing college sports, a foolish waste of time since we didn't know whether or not Dan would even be admitted to that school or if he would make the team.

Our conversation resulted in a triumph of brainstorming. We decided to wait and see what happened.

4. After you visit a college coach, your son or daughter should send a thank-you note. This is not mentioned in the NCAA handbook, but I think it's a nice touch and supposedly it keeps his name in their heads.

5. The only action we took next was no action. There are conflicting opinions about how aggressively to follow up on your visit. We decided to wait patiently for the coach to initiate any further contact. Pestering does not usually produce the desired results. We elected to call only if we had some monumental news item about Dan's tennis game to share.

6. Your child may be one of the lucky few to receive up to five all-expense-paid trips to visit one or several colleges that are interested in him. The NCAA handbook neglects to mention whether expenses are also paid for parent companions. No such offers came our way. We paid all expenses out of pocket.

7. There is something called a National Letter of Intent. This is a contract you must take as seriously as you do any other legal document. The NCAA brochure does not describe *exactly* what a National Letter of Intent includes, but I suppose if you sign it you are promising to participate in your sport should you be accepted into the college that sent it to you. I've never seen one of these letters close up. Having had no personal experience with it, I am unqualified to write about it. Parents of serious athletes always seem to know or find out what to do, so I wouldn't sweat it. If your child receives one, pour yourselves some champagne and congratulate yourselves on a sports investment that actually paid off.

Mr. Tennis Coach and Dan have been in touch by phone twice since Dan submitted his application. It is wonderful to have someone in your corner. As I write this, we are still in a "wait and see" mode. Since it's clear that scholarship money is not forthcoming, Dan can choose to play tennis or choose not to as the whim strikes him at the time. I am of the mind that he would be sacrificing much of what college is about in order to play sports. But I've never been an athlete. If I'd become the darling of the theater department, winning the diva role hands down for every university production, I would happily have sacrificed all of my afternoons and weekends to rehearsal and performance, regardless of parental advice to the contrary.

Dan will decide for himself if tennis is to be an integral part of his life in college. If he chooses it and is also chosen by it, I will send him home-baked cookies for the bus.

Chapter 16

Community Service Needed—No Wimps Please

Several months ago, I read an article in *The New York Times* written by a high school senior who aspired to go to Yale. At that time we did not yet know that it is possible to get C's at Yale and still get a job as President of the United States. This kid probably received his acceptance letter from Yale before the ink was dry on his paycheck from the "newspaper of record." The kid was not only fluent, but eloquent in written English, an asset that in itself sets him at least a century apart from his peers. I'd admit him to Yale in a heartbeat, even if his article had been picked up only by his community rag, instead of by the most prestigious paper in the country. His piece was about community service and the way it is performed by most of his peers in expensive East Coast private schools, which is begrudgingly and for the wrong reasons.

Community service—along with GPA, SAT, extracurricular activities, sports, essay, and recommendations—is a vital part of your child's personal college admissions profile. Colleges like to know that their student body is composed of socially conscious, philanthropically-minded young people. I have no argument with this. If parents fail to instill in their children a consciousness about helping those in need, preserving and protecting our environment, battling hatred, and promoting peace and diversity, then it becomes incumbent upon outside institutions to pick up the slack. Colleges do this by making you aware that they look favorably upon community service. Many high schools do it by requiring a minimum number of community service hours for graduation. Well, good for them. Children *should* grow up feeling that service to their community and the world at large is mandatory.

But—and this is what our young Yale hopeful wrote—the richer you are, the more your community service feels like a vacation. Being an umpire at community Little League games no longer counts as community service. Today, baseball leagues pay their adolescent umpires.

Community service today can mean traveling to Costa Rica to build houses and try hot air ballooning. It can mean traveling to Native American reservations to tutor children for a summer and fit in some good hiking and guacamole, too. Meanwhile, your next-door neighbor's house might have burned down and your kid doesn't even know they need clothing.

Plane fare to some of the exotic places today's kids select for their service activities can cost more than the value of the service they are providing. I understand the desperate need for tutors on reservations and sturdy houses in Costa Rica. It's admirable that American children by the DC-10 load are flocking to lend a hand. But is it the glamour or the real chance to do some good that attracts these kids to kindness? Yalie says it's the glamour. Yalie says his friends perform service only because it's required and not because of any internal moral imperative, so they might as well see the world while they're amassing good deeds.

Where does this leave a kid who lacks either the means or the maturity to embark on a philanthropic mission of this

106

Watsamatta U:
A Get-a-Grip
Guide to
Staying Sane
Through Your
Child's College
Application
Process

nature? Playing bingo with the aged at the nursing home is universally considered a "dorky" activity, I'm told. Yet I've never heard one of the wheelchair-bound residents call it that. Their eyes sparkle at the sight of a child, *anyone's* child, and volunteers earn affection and gratitude simply by walking through the door.

Charity has become a selfish act for many kids who are so overbooked with AP courses and sports and band practice and social engagements that they squeeze it in just because it looks good on the application. Yet, how many litter-strewn parks would remain dumping grounds if high schools didn't sponsor cleanup days whereby kids could earn valuable service points? How many fewer Habitat for Humanity homes would be built for deserving families? Kids may be coerced into giving, but at least the giving is accomplished and people benefit. Sad indeed.

I wonder how many young people continue to volunteer once they've won the admissions game and they're happily ensconced in college life. I hope it is more than I fear it is. Here in America, we do everything "big." Consequently, many of our children expect a "big" life replete with big recognition. Invisible, heartfelt giving to those close to home as well as to those oceans away must not become a thing of the past. *Random Acts of Kindness* has become a multimillion-dollar concept. I sincerely hope our young people catch onto it whether or not they accumulate points.

Dan fulfilled his community service obligations and surpassed them, which is a miracle because of his tennis schedule. He had to make choices. He enjoyed Habitat for Humanity, but couldn't participate as much as he would have liked because houses were built on Saturdays when grownups are off from work but tennis kids have matches and practices. If you want the tennis card, you need to play it out.

I would like him to have given of himself anonymously, the highest form of charity, but for him and others his age, this too has become impossible. Community service has become a part of the public record like everything else.

Ten Tips Regarding Community Service

1. Don't wait until high school to teach your children the value of giving of themselves to others. Very young children are ripe and ready for learning about helping those in need.

2. College lasts for four years, but life lasts a lifetime. Enrich your child's whole life. Embrace a cause.

3. Lead by example.

4. This is the one college requirement that makes sense in an impersonal world. Take advantage of it.

5. It should be a parental expectation for children to give of themselves. Let goodness be its own reward.

6. Remember: children are born good.

7. Match the service to your child's passions. Kids who love sports make great assistant coaches (provided there's no salary involved). Kids who love to sing are adored at nursing homes.

8. Join your child in his or her chosen philanthropy. My middle son and I work together once a week at the county shelter for abused women. I work on the hotline while he plays with the children of the residents. Afterwards we go out for dinner. Unlike college visitation, this is an intimate bonding experience. I relish this opportunity to forge intimate relationships with my children, one at a time.

9. Don't make your child sacrifice hobbies or too much free time in order to engage in service to the community. Teach him that service can easily fit into a busy life.

10. Millions of people volunteer on Christmas Day. If you can volunteer on an average Tuesday, you could make someone's day!

Chapter 17
Filling in the Blanks

I can easily understand why people would put off their first colonoscopy or going swimsuit shopping, but what in God's name is so heinous about filling in blanks on a college application form that kids insist on procrastinating until Federal Express has to get involved? You'd think they would fill in the darn blanks in a timely fashion just to get mothers like me off their backs!

Dan's "offsite" commitments suddenly and inexplicably tripled once it became time to actually sit down and fill out his applications. He was never home. He had either pressing concerns at the gym or tickets for a high school football game (a sport for which he'd never shown a scintilla of interest in the past) or an extra shift at work. Once he even went to the library to study rather than face all those ponderous and loaded application questions such as "When is your birthday?"

I'd like to say that our conversations from August to December added up to more than the sum of their parts, but they didn't. Their parts were annoying and ineffective and the whole was also annoying and ineffective. For five months my relationship with my son consisted of nothing but my nagging him to get off his lazy behind and start filling out forms and his responding with various and creative forms of communication, all of which expressed a single desire—"leave me alone." Which, of course, I ignored.

My solace during this period of time came from girlfriends who were suffering the same indifference from their children. Truncated conversations such as the ones Dan and I shared were apparently occurring throughout the neighborhood. It got to the point where my friends and I didn't have to ask each other for progress reports. We could read each other's eyes.

I bumped into my friend Nancy at the mall one day. This is what we said with our eyes:

Me

Hi. I'm so miserable. Dan is trying to bring me to my knees by refusing to even *start* his applications. They've been collecting dust on his desk for two months!

Nancy

I understand completely. Lauren won't even speak to me about it. I think she enjoys seeing how far she can push me before I crack.

Me

I've wiped this town clean of Mint Milano cookies. Look at me. I've worn these baggy overalls every day for a week. I can't button anything else.

Nancy

I'm living on Ben & Jerry's myself. It's the only way to get through it. Did Ben and Jerry go to college? I bet Ben and Jerry didn't even go to college.

Me

So what's the worst that can happen? He won't fill out his applications and he'll have to live home for another year and we'll have to start this whole thing over again.

110

Watsamatta U:
A Get-a-Grip
Guide to
Staying Sane
Through Your
Child's College
Application
Process

That's not so terrible.

Nancy

So what's the worst that can happen? She won't fill out her applications and she'll have to live home for another year and we'll have to start this whole thing over again.

That's not so terrible.

Nancy and Me

Yes it is! It's terrible! I've got to get home. I'm behind on my nagging.

This is what we said out loud:

Me

Hi. Gee, I'd really love to chat, but I'm late for a hair appointment. Call me soon!

Nancy

I'm late for work. I dashed over here to pick up a pair of pants for David. I'll call you soon. Dan doing OK?

Me

Same. Lauren?

Nancy

Same. Bye.

Me

Bye.

In public our eyes said what we couldn't bring to our lips, but into the wee hours of the morning, after our husbands threatened to divorce us if we uttered one more word about college applications, we would commiserate by phone. We'd compare the minutiae of our experiences with our kids, word-for-word conversations, and frustrations over B-plusses that, with the teeniest bit more effort, could have been A-minuses. Around and around in circles we would talk for hours, as if we were trying to solve the school violence crisis or explain how

Foucault's Pendulum works. I can laugh about it now, but months ago I couldn't have lived without the support.

There are two ways to fill out college applications now. You may fill out a paper application the old-fashioned way or you may submit applications via the Internet. There are numerous ways to screw up either kind of submission. The first can be ruined by bad handwriting or improper spelling, the only solution for which is requesting a new application and starting over. Electronic applications can be corrected instantly without having to begin again, but Adam, a friend's son, may have committed application suicide by clicking on a space that said "continue," which he thought meant that more application was to follow, but which really meant "send." He sent a hastily completed application that hadn't been proofed. He had even included a sarcastic response or two, which had made the process more enjoyable for him, but which he had planned to soften before sending. Too late. One second after clicking that mouse, the application is sealed. Retrieval is impossible. Some admissions officer is going to think Adam is just a wee bit out of line. For this reason, as well as my general, irrational distrust of technology, I encouraged Dan to fill out paper applications manually. It wasn't fun.

On an evening in November when HBO was in a slump, Dan decided, all on his own, to grapple with his first application. The first, of course, is the most time-consuming because you must compile your list of activities and honors and courses taken and current courses, which you can then simply copy onto your remaining applications. Dan spent a productive hour or so in his room, quantifying his life. As I'd suggested, he filled out the form lightly *in pencil* first, then proofread it, and finally traced over his writing with a good pen.

His big mistake occurred in step two, proofreading. He trusted himself to proofread his application, which was a very bad move. A pigeon would have to do his business on the

Watsamatta U:
A Get-a-Grip
Guide to
Staying Sane
Through Your
Child's College
Application
Process

paper in order for Dan to notice that something was amiss.

When I proofed his effort a few hours later, I found that he had consistently misspelled the word "friend," as "freind." Unfortunately for Dan, he works at *Friend's* Bar and Grill. Unfortunately for him, he wrote about how his best *friend* came to live with us for a year. Unfortunately, he traveled abroad with *friends* last summer. Unfortunately, one of his goals in college is to make new and lasting *friends*. Fortunately, you can download applications for this school on the Internet. Dan would need twelve more. He developed a mental block around the word "friend." It was amazing to watch. He would spell it correctly four or five times, then revert to the old spelling for the last appearance of the word at the very end of the application. Harold and I suggested that he might want to get a good night's sleep and start over in the morning, but he had become a madman, fixated on working this bug out of his system. In the end, he fell into a *"friend"*-induced stupor and had to finish the application the next afternoon.

As the weeks passed one into the next, Dan was to learn lessons about meticulousness that no teacher had yet managed to impart. I have not imagined or embellished the following.

By the time you fill out four or five applications, you know the ropes pretty well. Other than the essay, the questions are pretty standard. For example, all of the colleges, in one way or another, ask if you:

◆ are in good standing in your high school

◆ have ever been convicted of a federal crime

◆ have ever been suspended or expelled from school because of drugs or weapons

Usually these three questions are worded in such a way that the answer is either always no or always yes. On the last of Dan's applications, the questions appeared as they do above.

Dan answered "yes" to the first question, then assumed that the second two would require the same answer and checked the "yes" box for each. Had I not proofread the application, he would have informed his first choice school, whose application he had saved for last so he would be a pro by then, that he was a federal criminal. I suppose you could kill two birds with one stone in this case by using your FBI "wanted" picture for the yearbook, but that's taking things a bit too far.

Along the way you hear charming stories of applications sent out without the requisite check and applications that students neglected to sign. Dan's guidance counselor told me that she saw one application on which the applicant spelled his own name incorrectly. Apparently, he went by a nickname and had never needed to know the spelling of his given name.

Filling out college applications gives your child an opportunity to look deep inside and see exactly how much moral fiber is embedded there. While it is virtually impossible to lie about your grades or whether or not you were inducted into the National Honor Society, it's easy to manipulate the truth about less significant matters, such as whether or not you were really team captain or just co-captain, or how many hours you spent tutoring the geometry-challenged, or if attending the spaghetti dinner qualified as being an active member of the Italian Club, or if faculty-student ratio actually *is* your primary reason for selecting that particular school.

One can only hope that most kids and most parents are forthright about their accomplishments. I believe they are. The truth is, the real moral dilemma comes after all the blanks have been filled in and all the lists have been compiled and the only section that remains is the dreaded essay.

Chapter 18

In 500 Words or Less

Mom

Honey, you've been sitting at the computer for hours and I see all you've written is one word, "Essay." What's the problem?

Dan

If you must know, motherrrrrr, the problem *iiiiisssss* that I have no problems.

Mom

Excuse me?

Dan

Three colleges want me to write about the greatest adversity I have ever faced. So like, what am I going to say ... my little brother borrows my sweaters without asking? That'll impress them.

Mom

I don't think they care about the specifics of the problem you choose, as much as they care about how you coped with it and what you learned from dealing with it.

Dan

I coped with it by bashing his ugly face in, and I learned from it that my brother has a really mushy face.

Mom

Very funny.

Dan

I'm not trying to be funny. I can't do this. This is a stupid question.

Mom

I don't think it's stupid, honey. They want to know how you cope with your challenges. It delights me that you think you've had a problem-free life, but I can remember some bumps in the road. Why don't you write about how your tennis game fell apart a few years ago and you stuck with it and worked through it, and now you're better than ever...?

Dan

OK. And while we're at it, let's just call the NCAA and tell them that I lost part of my game *in high school!* That looks good. That looks just great. *I don't think so,* Mom!

Mom

Well, why don't you write about that girl who ...

Dan

Don't go there, Mom. God, Richard Powers is soooo lucky. About three people in his family have died recently.

Mom

Well, I'd be happy to help you out by killing someone, but I'm afraid it would have to be *you* for saying something so incredibly callous.

Dan

You know I didn't mean it like that. This is just so haaaarrrrd...

It is indeed hard. How many college-bound young men and women have experienced true hardship by the ripe old age of seventeen? How many of those gain the perspective to learn from misfortune by the end of high school? Most kids are both

116

Watsamatta U:
A Get-a-Grip
Guide to
Staying Sane
Through Your
Child's College
Application
Process

smart enough to know what true adversity is and humble enough not to blow normal adolescent rough patches into three-handkerchief essays. Occasionally a child loses a parent or a sibling or survives cancer or some other unspeakable disease. A strong "adversity essay" is far too sorry a compensation for having endured that kind of travail in one's youth.

Many kids go with the "death of a grandparent" essay. According to two popular college manuals, this essay crops up constantly and crosses over economic, racial, and gender lines. Kids write about how a piece of them died with their favorite Pop-pop or Nana or Grammie, but that this is the natural order of the universe and it is a blessing that Pop-pop or Nana or Grammie is no longer in pain. Other kids write about broken hearts or the death of a pet. Imagine reading 4,000 dead dog stories in the course of a few weeks. I'd blow my brains out, giving my colleagues fodder for their essays should they ever desire to move on.

Many colleges ask for simple personal statements, a short essay that will help the admissions officer "get to know you." This gives your child a chance for real introspection, an opportunity to be creative, and a walloping chance to screw up. What if the colleges don't like the real you? What if they'd prefer a fabricated version of you, created in the image of John Glenn or Madame Curie?

How creative is too creative? How many guts are too many to spill to a total stranger?

How do you show yourself to your best advantage without being haughty? How humorous can you be without going over the top?

We did receive one valuable piece of advice for Jewish kids. Never, ever write that you arrived in Israel, kissed the ground, and felt like you were home. It's been done. Apparently ad nauseam.

Just thinking of a topic for the essay can delay the postmark on your child's applications by months. We suggested dozens of topics. Write about your family, your trip to Europe, your passion for the movies, your favorite movie, your goals, the next-door neighbors, tennis, music, being the oldest, religion, racism, ecology, woodworking, the weather, your favorite president, Hitler, orangutans, *Seinfeld*, the beauty culture, marriage in the future, *Star Trek,* the beach, welfare, MTV, something, anything, *justwriteawready*!

At about this point, the moral dilemma hits you on the head about as hard as a frozen Butterball turkey dropping from the sky. There are people whom you can *pay* to write your essay for you. There are essays you can download off the Internet. These shortcuts are very tempting to a tortured young soul who believes that no one will be interested in whatever it is he has to say in whatever fashion he says it. I don't know anyone who actually made use of these slimy opportunities, or at least I don't know anyone who admitted to it, but a friend told me that *she* knows someone who hired an essayist for a very reasonable $500. The person *she* knows doesn't care how her daughter gets into Stanford, just as long as she gets in. There will be plenty of time for moral development later. What a country!

Getting Dan to write the essay was the most fun I've had since my gum surgery in 11th grade. Washing the car suddenly became more urgent to him than ever, as did helping his brother with his homework and scraping the scum off the shower door with his fingernails. Dan called this the gestation period. I guess I was prescient when I was writhing with contractions and declared that I was pushing out an elephant. Elephants gestate for something like thirteen years, don't they?

Finally we issued an ultimatum. Harold and I were going away for the weekend to attend a cousin's wedding. Upon our return we would demand to see a completed essay for our review or there would be hell to pay. We didn't care if he wrote

118

Watsamatta U:
A Get-a-Grip
Guide to
Staying Sane
Through Your
Child's College
Application
Process

it in haiku, as he had thought he would for a second and a half, or in pig Latin. He had to write it.

He did. It was creative and funny and just a little bit risky. If the admissions person reading it stepped on a tack the day Dan's essay made it to the top of the pile, there's a chance he or she might not be in the perfect frame of mind for it. We found it delightful, but we generally find Dan to be delightful. We were particularly delighted that we didn't have to make him pay hell. We're not sure what that means.

Dan eventually crafted three essays, which he used for eight schools. Try as he might to cut and paste the first so that it would meet the requirements of the second through eighth, it couldn't be done without sacrificing a few minor elements, such as form and content.

(I'd be interested to know if anyone could turn an essay about the greatest adversity you've ever experienced into one about who should be person of the century.)

Kudos must be given to Northwestern once again, this time in the category of "Most Challenging but Creative Essay Requirement." (I bet Harvard has a pretty daunting application as well.) In order to apply to NU the applicant must address, in 500 words or less, two of the following questions:

a. Is there something unusual that you plan to bring with you to college? Explain why you have it and why it is so unusual.

b. Anatole France said, "If fifty million people say a foolish thing, is it still a foolish thing?" On what subject do you disagree with most people, and why?

c. What work of art or popular culture today, widely known or obscure, will be remembered a hundred years from today as a representative example of taste at the end of the 20th century? What do you like or dislike about the work you have chosen?

d. Imagine you have written a short story, film, or play about your last four years. Briefly describe a defining moment or thing, and how it affects the rest of your autobiographical piece.

They must also write a short answer to this question:

e. NU's most unusual tradition is the painting of a stone monstrosity known as the rock. Students take turns painting it with slogans promoting political views, advertising campus activities, or expressing personal feelings. If given the opportunity, what message would you paint on the rock?

I wonder how many kids choose the cheer, "Admit me!" to paint on the rock. It wasn't the essay requirement that caused Dan to eliminate NU from his list. It was the essay requirement *and* the fact that he didn't have quite the grades or scores to get accepted *and* the fact that we didn't have enough money to endow a chair or build a stadium.

I am not going to lie and say that I didn't edit Dan's essays for him. I'm a writer. I can't, in good conscience, let any written material leave this house if it is flawed grammatically. But I wouldn't have changed the content if Random House paid me to. It was so … Dan.

College admissions people love to tell you that an essay written by an adult jumps out of its envelope and dances pirouettes on their noses. They are experts at recognizing cheaters. I don't know about that. I've received letters from grownups that read like fourth-grade journal entries and I've seen beautifully executed pieces created by teenagers.

Finally, the blanks are filled in, the essay has been painfully pulled out from somewhere near the spleen, I think, the check has been written, and the envelope has been addressed. And look! You're still ten hours ahead of deadline! Only Valentine's Day makes your FedEx delivery person more ecstatic! Stories of banging on the window at Kinko's copy center at

120

Watsamatta U:
A Get-a-Grip
Guide to
Staying Sane
Through Your
Child's College
Application
Process

two in the morning or calling FedEx for an emergency pickup that costs the same as your mortgage payment are hardly uncommon. You've had half a year to prepare for this one mailing, half a year to have your child's application arrive first and be given full attention by an admissions staff not yet exhausted from weeding through as many applications as there are residents of Pittsburgh. Sadly, it is not to be. Your child's application will arrive with tens of thousands of others posted twelve seconds before deadline. Still, it is out of your hands. Kiss it goodbye and move on.

Yeah, right.

Chapter 19
The Waiting Game

I noticed two things the day after Dan's applications were mailed. Their names are Andrew and Zack. They are Dan's younger brothers, who received my undivided attention about as frequently during the college selection and application process as their names have appeared in this book. I have a hazy memory of one family dinner during which Andrew stood at his place, spaghetti dangling from between his teeth, and wailed in frustration, "Are we *ever* going to talk about anything else?"

Zack is eight years old and knows where Middlebury College is. In sixth grade Dan and his friends were required to learn the capitals of the fifty states. I used to drill them by naming the state and having them race to name its capital. I haven't checked, but Zack could probably do this with colleges just by having witnessed so many of our circular conversations. New Jersey ... Rutgers. Georgia ... Emory. Indiana ... Purdue. I thank God that neither of my younger sons reached a significant rite of passage during the six months I was involved with Dan. It might have slipped into the sands of time as unacknowledged by loved ones as my last haircut.

122

Watsamatta U:
A Get-a-Grip
Guide to
Staying Sane
Through Your
Child's College
Application
Process

Andrew's baseball season came and went last spring as Harold and I spent weekend after weekend visiting schools. Over and over again we offered to take the two younger boys with us. Somehow, a spring afternoon in a confined department of admissions at the University of XYZ lacked the appeal of pitching a doubleheader in our own township park or going to see the first *Pokemon* movie on opening day with Matthew and the other guys from second grade.

We've all survived the separations. Andrew and Zack don't seem to hold my single-mindedness during that time period against me. But the stack of "days I wish I could do better" is far taller than I would have liked it to be by now. I've told Andrew and Zack that sooner than they think, it will be their turn to swim with me in the murky waters of planning a future. It makes them want to barf.

I've learned numerous lessons through this experience, one of which is not to talk so much. The more friends you have who bear witness to your frantic antics, the more questions you will have to answer as the days of reckoning approach.

"Where does Dan want to go to college?" I was asked ad infinitum in the early months. I repeatedly wished for the *chutzpah* to reply, "Where do you think? Harvard. Princeton. Duke. Why don't you ask me which colleges he's *applying* to?"

Rudeness doesn't become me, so I became adept at rattling off the chosen schools as routinely as I tell my family we're having macaroni and cheese for dinner again.

Once everyone on your wedding invitation list, including those you haven't seen since the nuptials, knows where your child is applying, the next question to pop up organically is "Heard anything?" People who are your friends should know that as soon as you hear anything you want to share you'll share it. I am still being asked, "Heard anything?" about five times per week.

It's my own damned fault. I am an open book. I watched a Greta Garbo movie sometime in my early adolescence and, after scrutinizing her remarkable face and then looking in the mirror, I had a strong sense that a similar air of mystery would be way beyond my ability to cultivate. Suppressed emotion gives me that dirigible-on-the-verge-of-explosion look. So I spill ... big, sloppy globs of undigested angst to whomever will listen. You'd be surprised how many people will listen if you're also adorable, which is how I try to overcompensate. The penalty is that genuine, well-meaning people always follow up. They think they're being kind to check on your emotional progress. So I talked about college a lot ... roughly all of the hours I was awake, which wasn't nearly as many hours as I spent thinking about it, because you can think in your sleep.

I thought about it in strange ways. Sometimes (and this is most embarrassing), it would actually make me feel better to think of all the women I knew who suffered losses far more grave than a child not getting into college. I count among my dearest friends some women who are truly heroic. In any random sampling of mothers, there are bound to be a few who mourn for children felled by disease before they could realize any dreams, college or otherwise. My sample includes Joanne. In any random sample of mothers, there are bound to be a few whose children survive gruesome accidents of fate, whose futures are altered irrevocably by incapacity. My sample includes Elayne. And, in any random sample, there are mothers who must watch their children do battle with their own bodies against microscopic invaders and daily fight for the right to be granted another day. My sample includes Laura. These mothers will tell you that they love and laugh and cope the way any other mother would, but they pull me up short whenever I think of them. They give me perspective when mine is woefully out of kilter. I feel guilty using them without their knowledge, in order to gain my own equilibrium. But boy, it sure works!

124

Watsamatta U:
A Get-a-Grip
Guide to
Staying Sane
Through Your
Child's College
Application
Process

For a while I could be in the middle of a conversation with the UPS delivery man and college would pop into my head. I could be navigating the twists and turns of an Oscar-worthy movie and lose track of the plot because I stopped at my mental mailbox to collect rejections. How special it must have been for Harold those few times I would break from his embrace during our most intimate connubial moments to ask him if he thought applying "early decision" was really such a good idea because what if Dan changed his mind in February and it was too late to do anything about it?

The worst part of the wait, other than the fact that no one in your family wants to be with you, is the second-guessing. You can drive yourself and those around you right up a wall by ruminating incessantly on questions such as these:

1. I wonder if he would have been smarter to take regular-track courses rather than honors. I've heard that many colleges consider only your GPA, not the rigor of the courses it derives from. An A is an A, whether it's in Spanish IV Honors or plain old Spanish for dummies.

2. Is it OK to call and make sure they've received the application? (The answer to this is yes. Many schools have Web sites you can visit to check on the status of your child's application.) But calling? Questionable.

3. Maybe if he declared a major in animal husbandry he'd have a better chance of getting admitted than he does with a communications major. How many kids from around here want to major in animal husbandry? How many know what it is? He can always switch majors later. Or maybe he'll fall in love with a cow and stay in it. It was really stupid to declare a major in communications right off the bat.

4. Was his essay a little too off the wall? My friend's daughter's guidance counselor told my friend that her daughter wrote a fabulous essay, but it didn't answer the question. Did Dan sac-

rifice content for cleverness? Should he call to ask if he could submit another one? What if the admissions officer who reads his essay lacks a sense of humor? Dan is toast.

5. *Everyone* applies to the state universities because they are more financially doable. Does he have a better chance at a high-quality private college? Did he apply to enough of those?

6. Do they need kids from Pennsylvania in Michigan?

7. Do they mean it when they say not to send too many recommendations? Especially from a member of Congress or Colin Powell, who apparently is acquainted with three quarters of the students in this country? Thank God we don't know any members of Congress or Colin Powell. But were his teacher recs glowing enough? Was there even a shred of a negative comment? Could anything be misunderstood? ... Ohmygod! Did the teachers even remember to *send them?*

8. The school has a rolling admissions policy. Dan submitted his application really early and hasn't heard anything yet, even though some other kids we know have. Is no news good news?

And on and on and on.

Second-guessing is an exercise in futility. There is absolutely no way of predicting how a college will act upon your child's application. Sam's College may have one too many tennis players this year and need a golfer. That ridiculous distinction is what it has come down to in the new millennium. Everything you read and everything they tell you on your college visits confirm that the number of college applications is at an all-time high. There are simply too many kids and not enough beds! Not every baby boomer went to college. Some of us were in Vietnam. Some of us thought college a waste of time. But the vast majority of baby boomer children are expected to obtain a degree. Consequently, Harvard University is rejecting nine out of ten applicants this year. Consequently, the Ivy League's

126

Watsamatta U:
A Get-a-Grip
Guide to
Staying Sane
Through Your
Child's College
Application
Process

highly qualified, but rejected applicants will fill the classes in the second tier of schools. Consequently, those second-tier schools will have to reject students who would have been shoo-ins in the past. Consequently, those students will trickle down into the third tier of colleges.

And on and on and on.

My brother serves on the admissions committee for graduate school at an Ivy League school. He says reading twenty applications in a single sitting triggers an instant migraine. Very few people with mediocre grades apply to the Ivy League. Once you eliminate the 15 percent of cockeyed optimists who shoot for it despite a shoddy transcript, the only truly fair and sane thing to do is have a lottery. Weight the applicants to ensure diversity, because far more white applicants apply than minorities, and then randomly pick numbers. I think he's right. Plus a lottery would make a whole lot of parents a whole lot calmer once they accepted, not just in their heads, but in their marrow, that the process is truly out of their control.

The Waiting Game Game

Every hyper-involved, college-obsessed parent plays it. I know that people I haven't met play it because I've overheard it being played in restaurants—not just once but *three times!* These are the rules of the game:

1. It should be played after all applications have been submitted, but before any responses have arrived. February is an excellent time to play because winter depression adds to the fun.

2. Pick three sets of friends, each of whom has a child the same age as yours. Parents who have older children and have already learned from experience are automatically disqualified. Ideally, these three sets of friends should live in three towns, so among you you've amassed a large database of friends and acquaintances.

3. Invite these friends to your home for an evening or go out to a movie and dinner or just to dinner.

4. Over a glass of wine, initiate a conversation about college. This is the easy part. College occupies most of the frontal lobe by February.

5. Each parent is to think of ten or twenty friends or acquaintances, depending on how much playing time you have set aside. Next, moving counterclockwise around the table, each player is to determine the level of success attained by each of those ten or twenty friends or acquaintances. Success is a subjective measure, so a brief discussion may ensue about what exactly it means to be successful.

6. See which players actually know which college each of the people on his or her list attended. Chances are, no one will have *any idea* which person went to which college.

7. If anyone *does* know which friend received a degree from which college, spend a minimum of twenty minutes determining whether or not you could have guessed it. Make bold statements such as "You'd think a guy who graduated from Brown could afford a bigger house than that! The entrance foyer is only a single story high!" or "He's the CEO of his own corporation and he went to *that* party school in Florida! Jesus!"

8. Wait quietly for three minutes. Something incredible will happen without anyone suggesting that it might. *Everyone* will mention that one of the wealthiest people in their town *didn't even go to college!* This is why it's best to play this game with people from other towns. Every town, not just Bill-Gates-the-dropout's town, but *every town* has someone who is not a college graduate but who's setting the world on fire, thank you very much. Ours is a good friend. He is completely self-made. *And* he has a bright and beautiful college-educated wife. *And* he has two bright and talented college-bound kids of whom he is rightfully very proud. So there you go.

Watsamatta U:
A Get-a-Grip
Guide to
Staying Sane
Through Your
Child's College
Application
Process

9. Even though everyone at the table has kids who *will definitely* be going to college, naming these successful degreeless people seems to make everyone at the table feel better. So, enjoy dessert!

Chapter 20
So What Happened?

The first response Dan received was a rejection. It arrived in a large envelope and I knew it was a rejection because his best friend, who had already been accepted at that school, had told him that the word "congratulations" was splayed on the outside of his envelope.

Dan was out of town visiting this best friend for several days when the bad news arrived. He called every day to ask if the mail had been delivered and, with a lump in my throat the size of a mango, I told him it hadn't. I had decided to replace the envelope in the mailbox on the day he returned, allowing him to discover it himself. My weekend was miserable. I spent most of my time rehearsing the inevitable consolation scene.

When Dan returned on Sunday night and asked me one last time, "Are you *absolutely positive* it didn't come?" I was so depleted by feeling sorry for him that I no longer had the stamina to keep up the ruse. I turned over the non-congratulatory envelope and explained to him that I hadn't wanted to ruin his visit with his buddy by dropping this bomb. I wanted him to have the "amazing" weekend he'd set out to have when he

130

Watsamatta U:
A Get-a-Grip
Guide to
Staying Sane
Through Your
Child's College
Application
Process

started saving his shekels for it months before.

"Excuse me. Did it ever occur to you that maybe I'd *want* to be with my best friend when this news came in?"

He was not gazing at me with the boundless gratitude I'd expected for my unselfish act of motherly love.

"Did it ever occur to you that being with my best friend might have *helped*?"

No, it hadn't. I had foolishly and selfishly thought that being with his *mother* would help.

How many psychology articles had I read in recent years that claimed that peer support in adolescence, and maybe even earlier, is far more significant to a child than support from a parent? It's the hot topic in parenting literature now. Once a child becomes social outside of the home, and this occurs at a very young age, a parent's level of influence decreases dramatically. Peers become far more potent factors in personality development and remain that way. I am living proof. On days when I'm able to take an honest look at myself, I realize that all my pushing and prodding, all my manipulations and attempts at controlling the life of my child, were not purely for his benefit at all. *I wanted to look good before my peers!* It's an ugly truth.

The point is, I made a parenting decision based on a false assumption. I'd assumed that a mother's love would override any support or encouragement from a special friend. There's another mistake I won't be making again.

Dan was angrier with me for withholding information than he was devastated by the rejection. Devastation is an emotion that my son, thank God, has yet to experience. Naturally, he was disappointed, but he handled the situation with aplomb. He spent the evening quietly in his room. He let me soothe him with some clichés about it not being the end of the world. I think he thought it would make *me* feel better. By the next morning he was his old, "let's see what kind of fun I can have today" self. Most of our children handle rejection with grace—perhaps not at first, but with practice they improve. The kids who don't handle it well eventually move on with their lives also. I don't know of anyone who can trace his or her arrested development to the day the college rejection came in. Dan knew that throwing a hissy fit wasn't going to change the facts. Life is still good for him. Pass the pizza.

Just as we feel personally impaled by our babies' DPT shots, our children's disappointments in later years burn scars into our souls. I did Dan a disservice by projecting my own juvenile issues with rejection onto him. Most kids apply to a few schools knowing that they will be both accepted and rejected—and that the latter occurrence is not a reflection of their personal inadequacies, but simply a function of numbers.

As of the day I am writing this, Dan has tasted a little bit of all the possibilities. He was accepted at his safety school, deferred by his long shot, and rejected by two schools we'd hoped he could get into. He's heard nothing from his first choice, so we still don't know where he will be attending college. The outcome of this process is not important. After all, this book is not about Dan. He just lets me use his name in every sentence.

The day his acceptance to that unnamed safety school arrived in an envelope bearing the word "congratulations" on the outside was the first day in about ten months that I felt myself breathe normally. It was the first day in almost eighteen years that I decided the time had come to fully, completely, and wholeheartedly leave Dan alone. He will be going to college. My work is done.

Almost from that day, I felt infused by an enormous amount of time and energy that had been sucked up by eighteen years of *hyperparenting*. I wish I'd coined that word myself, but I didn't. I

132

Watsamatta U:
A Get-a-Grip
Guide to
Staying Sane
Through Your
Child's College
Application
Process

serendipitously heard it on the radio today, coined by a couple who wrote a book about how the most competitive sport in America today is not golf, but parenting. They didn't say anything I hadn't heard already about how all of our children are so overprogrammed they don't know how to simply play anymore. They're unable to appreciate nature without a bat or a ball or a lacrosse stick in their hands or skis or snowboards on their feet. They aren't allowed the luxury of sitting still and watching a big old fly wend its way up the windowpane.

Childhood itself has become a performance. We no longer procreate in order to create extra hands on the farm or in the family store. We procreate to give our dreams a second chance. We believe that just maybe, if we're super-vigilant and totally involved, the sum of our parts *can* make a better whole.

All of us know this already. So why don't we stop? Why couldn't I let my unfulfilled dreams waft into the air and reach heaven? Why was it so important to me that my children surpass my own meager accomplishments? I should have encouraged my children to forge their own paths, not try to fit their shoes into the prints I left on mine.

I have a strong feeling that the denouement of this story would be the same even if I had been a laissez-faire mom. Dan would be going to college if I hadn't intervened with teachers, if I hadn't gotten apoplectic over an occasional C on a test, if I hadn't nagged him to work harder, organize better, strive for success. It must be nothing short of divine intervention that keeps him from holding a grudge.

Story time. I have a dear friend named Laura. Laura has a daughter named Fanya. Fanya always hated school. Hated, detested, reviled all that institutionalized learning stood for, which for her meant arising too early in the morning, conforming to a crowd in which you may or may not feel comfortable, sitting upright at a desk in a brightly lit room, and being talked at by a teacher on automatic pilot. Laura tried everything—*everything*—to get Fanya to twist herself into a "regular" child. It could not be done. There is nothing regular about Fanya. (There is nothing regular about *any* of our children, except that many of them are actually able to adapt to school.)

Laura had to take "irregular" measures. Refusing to push her child into a breakdown, she instead withdrew her daughter from school after the seventh grade. She let her sleep. She let her cook her own vegetarian lunches and eat them over the course of an afternoon. She let her grow back slowly into the bright, happy child she had once been.

When Fanya became Fanya again, Laura began to homeschool. Voices from the outside were relentless. "You're crazy. You're unqualified. You're overindulgent," they scolded. Friends, neighbors, and even family were certain that, together, Laura and Fanya were ruining Fanya's life by taking the raw materials of success, such as superior intelligence, natural creativity, and a truly good soul, and using them to create a dependent young woman without any initiative. How would she ever learn to learn, they wondered aloud and accusingly.

What a surprise when, under her loving mother's guidance, Fanya blossomed, until, at the age of fifteen, she *requested* the opportunity to take courses at the local community college. She is now holding her own with the twenty-year-olds, taking as many courses as she desires within a timeframe that's comfortable for her. Moreover, unlike the vast majority of our school students, she is truly learning for learning's sake. What a concept!

Meanwhile, homeschooling is no longer viewed as aberrant behavior or the path of last resort for unruly square pegs. Millions of Americans whom most of us would consider mainstream are pulling their children out of institutionalized education for millions of different reasons. I am not. I know that a

134

Watsamatta U:
A Get-a-Grip
Guide to
Staying Sane
Through Your
Child's College
Application
Process

homeschooling mom is not someone I can be. But I know I can do a better job with regard to my kids' education than I have done in the past.

I am trying to be less controlling with my second son. This doesn't involve a simple change in behavior. It requires me to change a large part of who I am at my very core—and it is more difficult and painstaking than any challenge I've ever undertaken. The process demands that I become deaf to outside voices that bombard all of us daily with messages about what success means. The process demands that I silence my own inner voice, which is the combined voice of generations of admonishments to achieve, achieve, achieve—as if true, soulful happiness and peace has ever come to anyone through achievement alone. But I am resolute.

Mrs. Adler has a theory about why so many parents have become so crazy in recent years. It's one we've all heard before, but it bears repeating. There is a truth that many of us must face as we send our babies into the world to greet their adulthoods. The truth is that our children may not ever exceed our own financial or professional success. In America, this is almost heresy. We are still a relatively new nation built by immigrants, most of whom forged for themselves and their children a better life than their parents had been able to provide for them. Today we live in an economic climate where "the millionaire lives next door." Prosperity is widespread. The poor have become invisible to the privileged. But the mindset changes ever so much more slowly than reality. In our minds we continue to push our children to exceed our own accomplishments. We want to eat their dust, even if it means we all will choke.

Mrs. Adler has been a guidance counselor for thirty years. Only in the last several has she seen a rise in migraines, ulcers, anxiety attacks, digestive problems, depression, and eating disorders that has gone from the dramatic to the frightening. Of course there are numerous societal factors other than parental pressure that contribute to the aforementioned problems in our young people. But that fact doesn't exempt us from accepting responsibility for whatever portion of the blame belongs to us. What will it take for us to stop making our kids sick? Many of them do a fair enough job of it without our help. It is incumbent upon us to change, to let our children know what we know but don't often show ... that our love is truly unconditional and that no one—*no one*—knows the secret ingredients for a bright future. If we did, we'd all be living ours.

Three months ago, I told Andrew, my second son, who is currently in ninth grade, that I would no longer be the homework Gestapo. In fact, I was going to disengage completely from all threatening conversation, which meant I would no longer bring up the subject of school. (Like Dan, Andrew is not exactly giving himself ulcers by working too hard.) I told him that I would not ask if his homework was completed or if he had a test coming up. I would not ask what his grade was on any test. I would not demand to tutor him or quiz him. I would only ask for his report card at the end of every marking period. Any school-related discussion would have to be initiated by him. For once, Dan did not consider his birth order to be an advantage. This year, Andrew is getting all the breaks.

The good news is that reinforcement is positive and immediate. Andrew and I have never gotten along so well, nor have his grades ever been so ... not bad. For the first time in quite a while, we enjoy each other's company. We play Trivial Pursuit regularly and many times he learns things against his will. I am consistently impressed with his range of knowledge. He is the current reigning champion and I don't make it easy for him to win. Andrew has a delicious sense of humor, which he warms us with whenever we're not yelling at him. Lately, we've all been laughing a lot. This is the adolescence I want him to remember.

136

Watsamatta U:
A Get-a-Grip
Guide to
Staying Sane
Through Your
Child's College
Application
Process

I've bitten my tongue so much I could probably insert a silver tongue ring without getting pierced. But I often slip and chastise him for watching television or sleeping too late. The experts agree that there exists within adolescent males an undeniable need to do nothing for great periods of time. When mothers respond to the question, "What did your son do over spring break?" with a curt "Nothing," most of the time the answer can be taken literally. "My son quite literally did *nothing* over spring break." The fact that this is normal behavior hasn't yet deterred me from trying to alter it. I think about colleges and how they want kids to participate in sports and run student council and write to their congresspeople about policies that disturb them and rack up thousands of community service hours, and I can't stop myself from screaming, "*Get off the damn couch!*" But lately, I remind myself that Dan spent two years on the basement couch *and* had a life *and* got into college. So I apologize and we move on to the next lapse.

As for Zack, there are certain advantages to having children at an advanced age. By the time he is ready for college, I'll probably be in diapers. I'll be too concerned about whether my own physical needs are being met to care whether or not he remembered to mail his applications by the deadline. Deadlines are relative. So far neglect has helped turn Zack into the most easygoing of children. Perhaps, if I continue to be preoccupied with nonsense, he'll have nothing better to do but become a good student!

I am still shaky, and I can't say that I don't suffer periodic relapses. But I've come to believe that both college and life will take care of themselves. I believe there is a college for everyone. Dan will be happy wherever he goes because he is a happy kid. Friends who have survived this process before me have tried to share this invaluable piece of wisdom. I wasn't listening or was too self-absorbed to absorb it. So I repeat it: Dan will be happy wherever he goes. Most of our kids will be happy wherever they go. If they aren't, they don't have to stay there! None of this really matters. But try telling that to a mother like me, shopping the bookstore for the *College Handbook 2002*.

I now believe that my kids will be unique gifts to the world, regardless of their SAT scores or the colleges they attend or the career paths they follow. I wish it wouldn't have taken me so long. I was a really hard sell. I am, in the words of the authors I heard on NPR today, a recovering hyperparent. I suppose I will be for the rest of my life.

Chapter 21
Goodbye, Good Boy

In the last analysis, it is all about letting go. All of parenting is—and it stinks. Occasionally, I wonder if I immersed myself so completely in the administrative details of applying to college because the busywork provided a welcome distraction from the encroaching realization that my precious baby will be leaving. Prevailing wisdom says that, by the time your child is ready to leave the house, he or she has become so impossible to live with that you are ready to give him or her the boot. Not so in this case. I really like my son.

My mother wore her sunglasses for forty-eight hours straight the weekend I was dropped off at college. She wore them even though it rained. She wore them indoors, which is a great look for Jack Nicholson but a bit discomfiting on a non-celebrity suburban housewife from upstate New York. Other mothers managed to maintain dry-eyed composure as they smoothed new sheets stiff as toast on fifty-year-old mattresses soft as Camembert. Mine was a walking, decorating, disinfecting tsunami. She could have power-washed the gymnasium with her tears. It was embarrassing, to be sure, but Mom's melancholia also amazed me. This was what she'd wanted! We bought that Northwestern sticker before I even unpacked my typewriter.

Perhaps I hadn't been the depressed, miserable, impossible-to-live-with bitch I thought I had been. Or perhaps she actually liked me depressed, miserable, and impossible to live with. She held me in embrace for entirely too long before she took her place, industrial-sized box of Kleenex in hand, beside my Dad in the new station wagon that would become her billboard, to begin the long weep home.

Despite sweltering September heat made worse by the rain, I shivered as I waved goodbye to my childhood. A queasiness came over me that would have sent me into the bushes to be sick if I hadn't noticed seniors making out in there. I wept as I climbed the stairs to a bedroom that for the first time in my life would not be my own. Four steps from the door and ready to hurl, I was subsumed by a gaggle of freshmen on their nervous but merry way to check out the ice cream bar at the student union. Bye, Mom. Have a nice life!

Fast-forward twenty-seven years. I'm a tall woman, yet I look up to see my baby's face now. It's a face that gets shaved daily and occasionally a pimple or two gets caught in the razor and bleeds, but when my cheek brushes against his to go in for the kiss, I swear I can still smell Baby Orajel underneath the Polo cologne. His arms enfold me only when I beg for a hug or if he wins something. They are muscular arms that lift me off the ground and can carry me as effortlessly as I carried him from pillar to post, from errand to errand. When I stop short in the car, I still reflexively extend my right arm to help his seatbelt hold him in place. It's a ridiculous gesture. It is he who is in the position to physically protect now.

How did this happen? I clearly boarded the wrong train. I bought a ticket for the local and somehow I ended up on the express. How will I sleep at night when he's no longer tucked

140

Watsamatta U:
A Get-a-Grip
Guide to
Staying Sane
Through Your
Child's College
Application
Process

into the wrought iron bed he selected for his thirteenth birthday present?

A hell of a lot better than I do now. Until recently, by law he could drive only until midnight. So why did he consistently come home at three minutes after twelve? You can die a thousand deaths in three minutes. Shakespeare knew this in the 16th century, before they even had cars. I don't wait up for him any more. I *wake* up for him. I can be deep in a bacchanalian dream of passion and poetry and still awaken at the sound of his key in the door. Parenthood has granted me many midnights. I nursed him nightly for a year. I sang him to sleep and patted his back and rocked permanent grooves into the carpet. And I did it with the purest love I have ever known. But now he's big enough to get his own damn midnight snack.

It's not as if I know the slightest thing about his life anymore anyway. I already miss being the sun in his solar system. Missing him will not be an unfamiliar sensation for me. I'm accustomed to being excluded from the mundane occurrences of his life. His friends are with him in the next room as I write this. They are playing baseball using a lemon and a spatula. He hasn't even told them that is *our* game!

I want to know how he spends evenings with his friends, some of whom are girls. I know I will forever be witness to his personal triumphs and tragedies, but I want to know how he'll take his coffee when he develops his taste for coffee. I want to know what joke is sweeping the dorm or the office. These are the details I will never be privy to again. When I weep about losing him, I'll be weeping for the boy who will always be counted as one of my vital organs ... the little boy who needed me to smooth the toothpaste on his brush and field his questions about God and nature and old TV shows and entertain him on snow days.

God, I hated snow days! Those days when schools are closed for no good reason except five inches of ice on the streets .... They claim the school bus drivers are afraid of getting stuck on the road. Getting stuck on the road would have been a picnic to me compared with being trapped in my house with three young boys and only *Home Alone II* for entertainment. The whining, the fighting, the 2000th game of Candyland—any of these by itself could give Harriet Nelson the shingles. I've shoved the memory of snow days into the darkest caverns of my brain, where even ginkgo biloba dares not go. God, I wish I could have some more of those snow days I hated!

I will be weeping for sure when I leave Dan on campus. And there is nothing at all I could have done to either prevent or prepare for this feeling of dejection. In my pre-childbearing naiveté, I thought I could safeguard against this excruciating feeling of loss by cultivating a full life of my own apart from my children. I was a daughter of feminism and *I had options!* I marched in Washington to protect my options, to ensure that I would never be a slave to a child I wasn't prepared to mother.

I worked for ratification of the ERA in order that my sisters and I might develop careers as rewarding, both personally and financially, as our male counterparts. I would never let my children become the center of my universe as I had become for my mother.

And then I had my children.

I am still a daughter of feminism. I am the woman I am because of the women's movement. Options for me were so much more plentiful than for my predecessors that one of them was actually to stay at home where I could be a mother and a writer simultaneously. I volunteer at a hotline for battered woman and I lecture and I teach and I make dinner parties. Every woman I know keeps a schedule as full as mine. But we are all mothers first. Declared feminists or not, working at home or outside, piling on volunteer activities six days a week,

Watsamatta U:
A Get-a-Grip
Guide to
Staying Sane
Through Your
Child's College
Application
Process

or commuting to big-city jobs, mothers groping in the dark for pieces of themselves and mothers who are at home with their most authentic selves, none of us can mitigate against the bittersweet blow of a child's coming of age.

Why can't I dislike him just enough to want him to leave? There were periods during the last seventeen years when I counted the years I had left before I could, in good conscience, send him into the world. But, I won't be sending into the world that boy child who forces me to sit through lowbrow movies such as *Ninja Turtles* three times in a row. I won't be sending into the world that petulant little boy who treats his little brothers like kelp that washed up on the beach just to annoy him. I won't be sending into the world that self-absorbed adolescent who doesn't know that sentences can begin with a word other than "I." Those incarnations, the Dans from whom a vacation would have been considered self-help are available to me only on video now. They've been replaced by a young man who shares his thoughts generously, who enjoys a good drama, who makes me laugh, who has always had my love but who has also earned my respect and my trust. In his eyes I see the glimmer of the man he is to be. I want to get to know this man … but it is time for him to leave. *Where is the justice in that?*

Dan will leave home shortly after my forty-fifth birthday. For a present, I guess I'll ask for a really cool pair of shades.

Chapter 22

A Chat with Other Moms

A s I typed the table of contents of this book and prepared to send it off into the publishing world for a good, healthy dose of rejection, my mind turned, as it always does at this point in the process, from the creative to the practical. As sure as I needed to be when I began this confessional, that the country is crawling with other mothers just as crazed as I was by the college selection and admittance process, I suddenly became wracked with worry that I am, in fact, a singular case of maternal hyperinvolvement. No other mother suffers the same angst over her child's future. Marketing this book will be impossible.

Well-equipped to be equally hyper in all areas of my life, I decided it was absolutely essential to the integrity of this endeavor to find out if other mothers could relate to my story. To this end, I held a round-table discussion in my home to discuss common and not-so-common experiences. I invited women from all areas of my life. Some were my best friends; some I hardly knew. We varied politically, religiously, and chronologically, not to mention in hairstyle. There were two major areas of commonality. All twenty-three of us were nes-

144

Watsamatta U:
A Get-a-Grip
Guide to
Staying Sane
Through Your
Child's College
Application
Process

tled comfortably in the middle to upper middle class and all of us had children who had been through the college selection process.

We gabbed for hours. Everyone had a story or two to share. Some of them follow.

Only Anna said she had little or nothing to do with her son Joe's college application process. "There is a reason for that," she hastened to add.

The family lived in Germany for three years where Joe attended a German school and was treated miserably by the other kids and received little if any help from the teachers. He had no choice but to become very independent. Once they returned to the States, when Joe was in high school, he had established a pattern of self-reliance. Plus, he was so happy to be back, he exceeded all academic and personal expectations. For extra measure, he received a five (the top score) on the AP German exam.

Anna fully expects to be as involved as the rest of us were when it comes time for her second son to begin his own search.

The rest of us, whether born with natural proclivities toward anxiety or not, went nuts. We all nagged. We all helped with applications in one way or another, either by taking days off from work to type essays and extracurricular lists, like Sharon, or by proofing, stamping, editing, or mailing late into the night. Did I mention that we *all* nagged?

All of us had kids who procrastinated, some to the point of total dysfunction.

Candace, after months of nagging, formulated her own explanation for this. "It's very clear and simple," she said. "My son does not want to face the inevitable. He loves his family, his school, and, most of all, his friends. The thought of leaving all that he loves behind for an unknown is more than he can handle. His procrastination has nothing to do with laziness. It has everything to do with fear."

Heads nodded around the room. Of course. *Of course.*

Amy became a single mother when both her sons were very young. When her son didn't jump at the chance to go college shopping, she was perplexed. Then she met a man with whom she developed an intimate, long-term relationship. Suddenly, it became OK for her son to prepare to leave home. His mother would be OK.

Janet had a friend who became a widow last year. Her son, wracked with guilt over leaving her alone, is unable to face the thought of going to college.

We watch our children work to the rhythm of their own internal metronomes for so long and for such ludicrous reasons—"I can't do homework now because I burned my tongue"—that it is understandable that we sometimes miss the signs of legitimate, anxiety-induced procrastination. Poor babies. As mothers, we think our anxieties about our children would be alleviated if only they would get off their behinds. Sometimes, lying on one's behind is exactly what one must do to stave off anxiety.

Exactly zero of us had children who chose a college because of the faculty-student ratio. Elayne's daughter chose her school because she liked the dorm room. When she was miserable at that school, she chose her new one because her best friend was there. Brenda's daughter never saw the school her boyfriend attended, but decided to forgo her lifelong interest in marine biology in order to follow him to a landlocked campus.

Zero of us had the wonderful bonding experience we had planned to enjoy on the college visits. Janice took her son's girlfriend along. Big mistake. They had a great time, but they

Watsamatta U:
A Get-a-Grip
Guide to
Staying Sane
Through Your
Child's College
Application
Process

would have had that same great time at the University of Timbuktu. They barely noticed the environment.

When Judy awoke on the rainy morning her son took the SATs, she hit the panic button upon noticing that he had left his calculator on the kitchen table. Off she went in her pajamas to an unfamiliar private school twenty minutes from her home to bring it to him. When she arrived, she found that the school was not housed in a single building. Soaking wet and in tears, she trod in her muddy pajamas from building to building in search of her absent-minded child. As she told us her story, I pictured Scarlett O'Hara in the mud of war-torn Atlanta, falling to the ground and swearing she would never go hungry again. When Judy finally found the proctor of her son's exam, she was told that he wasn't allowed to give her son his calculator because it would disturb the other students. She begged him for consideration and left him with the calculator. Upon her son's arrival at home three hours later, she asked if he had been given the calculator.

"Yes, mom, but there were no batteries in it. I took them out to put them in the calculator that I brought with me!"

And, speaking of proctors, Ruthellen's oldest daughter's proctor suffered a heart attack while she was taking the LSAT. Students had been warned in advance of the test to not let *anything* distract them from successfully completing the exam in the time allotted. This poor man moaned and clutched his chest and dropped his head on his desk without anyone looking up. Finally, a relief proctor arrived, according to procedure, to give the proctor a time out. He sized up the situation and immediately called 911. In ran the paramedics. Down went the proctor. CPR was administered. Nary a student lost a precious test-taking moment. They would each be damned if they'd let a heart attack gyp them out of valuable points. In three years this will be our new generation of lawyers.

Later, when some of the students asked that the results of this test be discarded and that a new test be administered at a later date, their request was denied. Good Samaritanism suffered a major setback that day. Why *should* those kids have come to the aid of a total stranger? They certainly didn't need any community service points. And the system would have penalized them if they had succumbed to what I optimistically believe is a natural human instinct to help one another. Why aren't we rethinking the system?

The mothers in my family room took no notice of the hours ticking by. My chocolate chip cake and homemade biscotti sat on the table untouched until someone declared it was 10:00 already. Still the stories spilled out without coaxing.

Janice's son messed up his Social Security number on his application. That number is used to differentiate you from the other 25,000 applicants at a particular school. She had to run interference with the admissions officer.

Janet's son forgot to take one whole test when he sat for the SAT IIs.

Sharon's older daughter took private tutoring for the SATs and managed to lower her score by 200 points. She was so worried about remembering all the little memory tricks he'd taught her that she forgot all the information she used to know. She is now a successful high school *and* college teacher.

The mothers who had been through this before with older children tried to tell the rest of us that none of this mattered. Ruthellen, whose daughter has to take a plane to school, was able to have lunch with her daughter twice in four years. Linda, who kept her children within an hour's drive of home, saw her daughter about as often.

Those of us going through this for the first time swear we won't be so crazed with the second child. The veterans tell us we will.

Watsamatta U:
A Get-a-Grip
Guide to
Staying Sane
Through Your
Child's College
Application
Process

Maybe.

"Could we have done it differently?" I asked as I handed each mother her coat. "Could we have not taken it so seriously?"

Maybe.

No.

Photo by Elayne Klein

Karin Kasdin is an award-winning playwright and author. Her book, *Oh Boy, Oh Boy, Oh Boy: Confronting Motherhood, Womanhood and Selfhood in a Household of Boys*, was named outstanding parenting book of 1997 by The Parent Council Ltd.

Her other books include *Disaster Blasters: A Kid's Guide to Being Home Alone* and *Food No Matter What: Stories and Recipes for Perfect Dining in an Imperfect World*, both co-authored with Laura Szabo Cohen. Ms. Kasdin's plays have been produced in regional theaters, and her articles have appeared in national magazines.

She resides in Bucks County, Pennsylvania with her husband and three sons who are thankful that they don't share her last name.